BBQ

A Wiley Brand

BBQ

by Carey Bringle

BBQ For Dummies®

Published by: **John Wiley & Sons, Inc.**, 111 River Street, Hoboken, NJ 07030-5774, www.wiley.com

Copyright © 2021 by John Wiley & Sons, Inc., Hoboken, New Jersey

Published simultaneously in Canada

For general information on our other products and services, please contact our Customer Care Department within the U.S. at 877-762-2974, outside the U.S. at 317-572-3993, or fax 317-572-4002. For technical support, please visit https://hub.wiley.com/community/support/dummies.

Wiley publishes in a variety of print and electronic formats and by print-on-demand. Some material included with standard print versions of this book may not be included in e-books or in print-on-demand. If this book refers to media such as a CD or DVD that is not included in the version you purchased, you may download this material at http://booksupport.wiley.com. For more information about Wiley products, visit www.wiley.com.

Library of Congress Control Number: 2021932827

ISBN 978-1-119-59245-7 (pbk); ISBN 978-1-119-59225-9 (ebk); ISBN 978-1-119-59228-0 (ebk)

Manufactured in the United States of America

SKY10026914_050721

Contents at a Glance

Recipes at a Glance

Rubs

Brines

Marinades

Sauces

Side Dishes

Desserts

Table of Contents

Introduction

B arbecue, also known as BBQ, Q, 'que, and yum delicious, is a way of life for the lucky few. I am certainly one. I wrote this book to share my love of this uniquely American cooking technique.

I grew up with barbecue, so for me, it's a very familiar topic. But even if you're just starting out, this book is ideal for you. I walk you through the tools, tips, and techniques you need to adopt this wonderful hobby that I chose to make my profession.

The barbecue life is about family and friends and sharing with them your love of cooking and good food. Because this style of cooking takes a long time, it gives you the opportunity to spend time with the people you love. True lovers of the barbecue lifestyle also embrace sharing with others and passing the knowledge they've gained along the way to the next generation — which is why I wrote this book. I'm not writing to preach to you about my life experiences and accolades but rather to share with you a world that has brought me great joy in the hopes that it'll do the same for you.

Barbecue is for everyone, and this book is no different. Barbecue brings together people of all walks of life. Embrace the differences in other people's barbecue, and discover your own style through trial and error. Your heart will lead you in the right direction. Now get out there and get to smoking!

About This Book

BBQ For Dummies offers my expert take on all things barbecue, from how to find a grill or smoker to the tools you need to methods for preparing the meat to delicious recipes for actually cooking the meat (and some vegetables, too).

In this book, I give you the basics: the temperatures you need to know, the cuts, the cookers, the techniques, and the tools. Use this book as a handy guide to getting started in barbecue. This book is a beginner's guide, but it also has some topics for the more advanced, so even if you think you know everything there is to know about barbecue, this book is for you!

Cooking barbecue isn't rocket science, but it can be a personal struggle to be patient when smoking. In fact, being patient may be the hardest part. Don't let your enthusiasm for what you're cooking lead you to ruin your cook through lack of patience. If you follow the techniques and temperature guides in this book, you'll soon find your groove and be the pit star you were meant to be.

I've been cooking barbecue for over 35 years. Some things I was taught, and some things I learned on my own. In this book, I pass that knowledge on to you. When you finish with this book, it can still act as a guide for the temperature and techniques that will bring you back to the basics of great barbecue.

Here are a few ground rules relating to the recipes:

>> All oven and cooking temperatures are measured in degrees Fahrenheit; flip to Appendix B for information on converting temperatures to Celsius.

>> All eggs are large.

>> All onions are yellow (unless otherwise noted), but feel free to use Vidalia or white.

>> For measuring purposes, dry ingredients are lightly spooned into a standard U.S. measuring cup or spoon and then leveled with a knife. Liquids are measured in glass, standard U.S. measuring cups. Check out Appendix A if you need help converting to metric measurements.

>> All sugar is granulated.

>> All flour is all-purpose.

>> The term *lightly browned* indicates when the food just begins to change color.

>> All herbs are dried unless specified as fresh.

>> Lemon and lime juices are freshly squeezed.

>> All ground pepper is freshly ground black pepper.

>> References to *percent daily values* or limits on nutrients are based on a daily intake of 2,000 calories.

>> Recipes marked with the tomato icon (🍅) are vegetarian.

Anything marked with the Technical Stuff icon you can safely ignore. You can also ignore the stories in the sidebars — they're interesting but not essential to understanding the topic at hand.

Finally, within this book, you may note that some web addresses break across two lines of text. If you're reading this book in print and want to visit one of these web pages, simply key in the web address exactly as it's noted in the text, pretending as though the line break doesn't exist. If you're reading this as an e-book, you've got it easy — just click the web address to be taken directly to the web page.

Foolish Assumptions

My basic assumption about you, the reader: You want to know more than you do about the low-and-slow cooking method that produces mouthwateringly delicious barbecue.

I also assume you're familiar with cooking in general, but for the purposes of this book, I assume you know very little about cooking barbecue. I also assume that you're ready and able to develop the patience cooking good barbecue requires — remember, low and sloooow.

Icons Used in This Book

The little images in the margins draw your attention to relevant info. Here are the icons in this book:

TIP

Actions that can make your barbecue life a little easier get the Tip icon.

REMEMBER

The Remember icon highlights points to keep in mind as you hone your barbecue skills.

WARNING

In cooking barbecue, you build fires, and fires can be dangerous. Pay attention to text marked with this icon, which tells you what to avoid.

TECHNICAL STUFF

The rare Technical Stuff icon points to information you can skip. The text here explores technicalities that aren't essential to know.

Beyond the Book

In addition to what you're reading right now, this product comes with a free access-anywhere Cheat Sheet that includes info on barbecue styles in the United States and barbecue competitions. To get this Cheat Sheet, go to www.dummies.com and type **BBQ For Dummies Cheat Sheet** in the Search box.

Where to Go from Here

You can read the chapters of this book in any order you like. Each chapter stands alone in giving you the vital information you need for that topic. Feel free to bounce around and explore what particularly interests you at the moment. There is no particular right way to learn this information, but it's all in here for your quick and easy reference.

If you're a complete novice and just have an interest in barbecue, start with Chapter 4 on grills and smokers and decide how big or small you want to go. Then browse Chapter 3, the tools section, to make sure that you have what you need to get started.

For the amateur who already has a setup and has started experimenting, you may want to start with meat cuts to get a better understanding of what's out there to choose from. The new cut you hadn't heard of or didn't know how to use may become your new favorite.

Jump around! Look for the areas where you feel you need improvement. The book is not linear — it's a reference for you to keep near your smoker.

Finally, keep one very important thing in mind: Have fun! Barbecue is meant to bring people together. True members of the barbecue family understand that keeping secrets about methods or having arguments over techniques are counter to the core of barbecue. Enjoy the cook, and work to bring others into the world we love so much!

1

Getting Started with Barbecue

Dig into the history and methods of barbecue, including touring the various types of barbecue across the country.

Get into the particulars of cooking low and slow, which is the basis of cooking authentic barbecue. Putting meat on the grill at a low temperature for a long time — I'm talking hours, not minutes — is how you produce great barbecue.

Gather the necessary equipment, and tools that are just fun to have. You need a cooker, tongs, a thermometer, and some fuel to cook barbecue. You may also want a spray bottle, a basting brush or mop, and a grill screen. Find all the tools you need and discover others you just want.

Roll out the qualities of a great smoker or grill. Run through the types and formats of various cookers and decide on the one you want. Then make sure your choice has the quality to keep you cooking barbecue for many years to come.

IN THIS CHAPTER

» **Looking at the origins of barbecue**

» **Traveling through the key regions**

» **Getting into method**

» **Assembling everything you need**

» **Making barbecue**

Chapter **1**

Taking a Closer Look at Barbecue

As long as humans have had fire, they've been cooking meat over an open flame and eating barbecue. Barbecue is the great equalizer. Politicians use barbecue to rally people to their causes, and barbecue has brought people together in social gatherings for well over 200 years. No matter your race, color, creed, or religion, you can gather with your family and friends around a table and enjoy a great meal of barbecue.

Barbecue Beginnings

Ah, how it all began. I guess you could say that the first time a cook put a piece of meat over a live fire, barbecue was born. No telling when that was.

Barbecue has many definitions and meanings all around the world. In the United States, *barbecue* is defined as meat cooked at a low temperature for a long period of time using wood or wood charcoal as the primary heat source. In many other parts of the world, it may be just grilling meat over wood either hot and fast or low and slow. In some areas, it may be stewing in a pot over wood coals. One thing that is a common trait is that wood or wood charcoal is always involved. In Australia, it may be iron wood; in California, fruit wood; in Tennessee, hickory.

The popularity of barbecue has swelled and retracted and swelled again. Fortunately, in recent years, a resurgence of artisanal barbecue has taken place, with folks doing it the old-fashioned way and new restaurants sprouting up all across the United States.

Barbecue in the United States and abroad

As far as modern-day barbecue is concerned, Christopher Columbus encountered it when he came to the new world in 1492. Indigenous people were cooking meats over an indirect heat source of green wood, which allowed the meat to cook without burning and to cook low and slow. The Spanish-speaking people refer to this as *barbacoa* — what we now refer to as *barbecue*.

This low-and-slow technique was also witnessed by Hernando de Soto when he was treated to a feast by the Chickasaw tribe near what is now Tupelo, Mississippi, in 1540. From there, the tradition made its way to the colonies, specifically Virginia and the Carolinas.

In other countries, *barbacoa* or *barbecue* is meat hung over a direct live fire or a live fire pit to cook.

No matter where you eat barbecue in the United States, what makes it barbecue is that the meat has been cooked over wood or wood charcoal for a long time at a low temperature.

From humble beginnings to art form

Barbecue was born from humble beginnings. Plantation owners took the best cuts of meat from the hog and left the toughest pieces of meat for the men and women they enslaved. The method of cooking these tough cuts at a low temperature for a long time — low and slow — helped take a very tough piece of meat and turn it into a tender delicacy.

The traditional method of cooking barbecue involved either making a pit with brick or stone and cooking the meat over coals or digging an actual pit in the ground, filling it with coals, and cooking the meat on top of that fire.

Over the years, barbecue has evolved. It went from holes in the ground to stone pits; then to brick pits, smokehouses, metal pits, gas-assist pits; and now even wirelessly controlled pellet pits. A lot has changed over the years. One thing remains constant: Fire is the element that ties the evolution of barbecue and the tools used.

As of late, due to the increasing popularity of sanctioning bodies and competitions on cooking shows, barbecue is popping up all over the United States, with thousands of enthusiasts located in various regions across the country. In fact, barbecue has become such a phenomenon in the United States that excellent barbecue places are now popping up in areas that traditionally never had a barbecue heritage.

Going for a Regional Spin

Barbecue tends to be a tradition throughout the South, but four premier regions known as the Barbecue Belt really define barbecue in the United States: the Carolinas (North and South), Kansas City, West Tennessee, and Texas. That's not to say that there isn't great barbecue all around the country. More and more great barbecue joints are popping up everywhere, but these regions, more than any other, really define the nature of barbecue in the United States.

I look at each of these regions (and some others) in the next sections, talk about the distinct flavor profile of each region, and fill you in on what each considers true barbecue.

The Carolinas

Although the Carolinas started out as one province, the area was settled by people from all over Europe, leading to several distinctive barbecue styles in the two modern-day states. I explore these differences in the following sections.

North Carolina

North Carolina is known as the first region in the United States with a distinctive barbecue style. North Carolinians started eating barbecue very early on in the country's history. The barbecue tradition expanded from here west to other regions, including West Tennessee, Texas, and on into Kansas City.

In a state defined by barbecue, North Carolina has not one but two distinct barbecue flavors and styles: an eastern North Carolina vinegar sauce and a red, Piedmont-style or Lexington dip sauce.

GOING WHOLE HOG IN EASTERN NORTH CAROLINA

Eastern North Carolina is the land of whole-hog cooking. Typically the barbecue sauce used on that hog is vinegar based with added ingredients such as salt and pepper, red pepper flakes, or a hot sauce.

Sometimes the sauce is mopped on the hog as it cooks, but often the whole hog is chopped so that parts from all over the hog blend together sometimes even including the skin. After the meat is chopped and blended together, it gets doused in the vinegar hot sauce so familiar to the area.

Sandwiches are topped with a chopped mayonnaise coleslaw.

DIPPING INTO PIEDMONT STYLE

A Piedmont-style or Lexington dip sauce also starts with a vinegar base — apple cider vinegar to be exact. You add tomato ketchup and other ingredients to sweeten the sauce and give it a red color.

The Piedmont style isn't as sharp as the eastern Carolina style — it's more akin to a Memphis-style red barbecue sauce.

Lexington-style North Carolina barbecue is typically a whole shoulder of the hog — what's called a *pit dip*. The red sauce used in Lexington-style barbecue is typically also used for the slaw, in order to make a red slaw that tops a sandwich.

South Carolina

The style of cooking barbecue in South Carolina is similar to that of North Carolina, but mustard prevails thanks to the many German settlers in this area. Whether for whole-hog barbecue or pork shoulder, mustard sauce rules.

Mustard sauce is typically a yellow-mustard base along with apple cider vinegar and spices added to inject a certain level of kick.

TIP

If you have leftover barbecue in South Carolina, you make Brunswick stew. Barbecue hash also seems to be making a comeback in the region.

Kansas City

If West Tennessee-style barbecue and Texas-style barbecue had a baby, it might be called Kansas City. Kansas City is the first big region to marry two styles of barbecue into one uniquely regional style.

The Kansas City barbecue scene started when Henry Perry from Memphis moved to Kansas City in 1907. By 1910, he had saved enough money as a porter to open the Eat Shop, where he took the tradition of West Tennessee barbecue, which consisted of pork and chicken, and added in beef. That business later evolved to be Henry Perry – King of BBQ, and at one point he had three locations. Upon Perry's death, his apprentice Charlie Bryant took over; he later sold the business to his brother, Arthur Bryant. Bryant changed the name of the restaurant to Arthur Bryant's and the name remains today. Another protégé of Perry started the famous Gate's BBQ in Kansas City as well.

Kansas City barbecue is typically thick, sweet, and tangy. A Kansas City sauce starts with a tomato base but often adds ingredients like molasses, brown sugar, or even Worcestershire or soy sauce. The sauce tends to be a thick, dark, rich sauce familiar from most grocery-store brands.

Kansas City–style ribs are generally wet and sticky. The uniquely different burnt ends from the point of a brisket, doused in sweet and sticky sauce, make this a special region with multiple styles, including some of their own.

West Tennessee

West Tennessee barbecue is typically pork shoulder that's been slow-cooked, typically over charcoal, with a tomato-based sauce. Sometimes that sauce is sweet; other times it's tangy.

The West Tennessee–style sandwich is made with pulled pork topped with sauce and coleslaw. *Pulled pork* (pork cooked to a temperature that's hot enough to allow the meat to literally be pulled apart in your hands) originated in West Tennessee. (Meat's collagen breaks down at 192 degrees, and the absence of collagen makes it very tender.)

Cities in West Tennessee, including Lexington and Henderson, have a long tradition of whole-hog barbecue. To cook a hog Tennessee style, you need not one but two fire pits — one to burn the coals and one to cook the hog. You burn down live coals and then shovel the coals under the hog to smoke it.

The fire pit to make the coal can be a burn barrel or a separate chimney dedicated to burning down wood. A pit is usually crafted with a grated, elevated bottom so that the coals fall through. You put wood in the top, and the coals fall through the grated floor as the wood burns. You then scoop out the hot coals and shovel them under the hog.

The difference between a West Tennessee whole hog and Carolina hog is the fact that, in West Tennessee, portions of the hog are pulled off as they're requested. You may want part of the ham or shoulder or, if you really know what you're doing, you ask for some middlin' meat or belly.

These two different styles of cooking a whole hog produce two different results but make equally delicious sandwiches.

In Memphis, which is about as far west as you can go in Tennessee, the sauce is tomato based, typically with added ingredients such as apple cider vinegar, molasses, brown sugar, and other spices to make it a tad bit sweet or give it a tangy bite. A Memphis barbecue sandwich has sauce and slaw and is typically middle of the road with a hint of savory.

Texas

In Texas barbecue, beef is king. Texas is cattle country, and out of that tradition was born beef barbecue. They like to do it big in Texas, and they like big cuts of meat. Brisket is king, and beef ribs are the crown princes of barbecue there.

Texas barbecue is cooked low and slow, typically with a rub that consists of only salt and pepper and produces a product that is moist and juicy and melts in your mouth.

The ribs in Texas are different as well. They're beef short ribs or plate ribs, and one rib can be over a pound of meat. Cooked in the same tradition as brisket with a salt-and-pepper rub, ribs have a mouthwatering flavor and texture that is uniquely Texas.

REMEMBER

In most places in Texas, *sauce* is a dirty word. Barbecue is sliced, put on a slab of butcher paper, and served with no sauce in sight. To Texans, the meat either stands on its own or doesn't stand at all.

Other important players

Barbecue is a cultural phenomenon second only to apple pie or baseball. You don't get more American than barbecue, and that comes in many different shapes and forms all around this great country. Barbecue's popularity has spread across the United States; it's not just the four premier regions anymore. Here are some examples:

>> **Alabama:** North Alabama has become a staple in the barbecue world, defined by the white sauce applied to a smoked chicken or turkey.

Alabama white sauce was made famous by Big Bob Gibson in Decatur, Alabama. (I include his restaurant in my ten-best list in Chapter 20.) It has a mayonnaise base and is thinned with either white vinegar or apple cider vinegar. The other ingredients include black pepper, maybe lemon juice, and sometimes sugar.

You can find many variations on Alabama white sauce with various ingredients — check Chapter 13 for my recipe. Experiment on your own and see what stands out to you.

>> **Georgia:** Georgia now has its own barbecue community defined by a mixture of different styles. Texas, West Tennessee, and Kansas City styles are all present in the Georgia market.

>> **Kentucky:** Kentucky has its own unique take on barbecue — mutton defines Kentucky barbecue to a T. Simply put, mutton is lamb barbecue, and it's unique to Kentucky.

The lamb is slow-smoked just like a pork shoulder, a whole hog, or even a brisket, and it's often pulled and coated with sauce.

TIP

When Kentuckians have leftover mutton barbecue, they make *burgoo,* a stew made with mutton barbecue very much in the tradition of Brunswick stew, which was born out of South Carolina barbecue.

I could go on to name almost every state in the country and talk about the different styles of barbecue there. You find distinct barbecue styles from California to New York. People have the barbecue bug, and they're coming up with their own spin on what was once a very narrowly defined American tradition. Generally, barbecue in states that aren't defined by a particular region or a particular style are an amalgamation of multiple styles of barbecue.

The abundance of different styles of barbecue — more than you can count — gives the citizens of the United States the unique opportunity to try a new style in almost every state they visit. Barbecue, simply put, is a great American tradition no matter which way you slice it or pull it.

Applying Heat to Meat, Slowly

Barbecue is all about time and temperature. The low-and-slow cooking process gives the meat time to break down its internal structure and become tender. Consistency in your heat source and enough time are key elements to this formula.

Smoke + heat = magic

With barbecue, smoke and heat make the magic. In order to have both smoke and heat, you need wood. That wood can be in the form of coals you burn down in a pit and shovel under your piece of meat. It can be in whole logs you put in a pit. You can use carbonized wood, commonly called *charcoal.*

For your smoke source, you can use logs, chunks, or chips. These three sizes of wood are readily available at most hardware stores. Logs give you the slowest burn of the three, chunks are next, and chips burn fastest. What you use depends on the type of smoker or grill you have and the size constraints. None of the three is preferred — you just need to understand that they have differences.

REMEMBER

Nearly always, you cook barbecue over *indirect* heat. You place the meat off to the side, not directly over the burning wood.

The one sure thing is that if you don't have heat and you don't have smoke, you don't have the great American tradition of barbecue.

Keeping it low and slow

Barbecue is not rocket science — no need to be intimidated. You may think you'll never master the craft of barbecue, but it's a very simple process.

REMEMBER

Barbecue takes time. It takes the right temperature, and it takes consistency. If you have the patience to make sure that your barbecue cooks for the right amount of time at the right temperature consistently, you can make great barbecue.

You need to be aware of some key temperatures when you cook barbecue:

>> **Cooking temperature:** Traditional barbecue is typically cooked at a temperature between 190 and 250 degrees. A good middle-of-the-road temperature to aim for is 220 degrees.

>> **Internal temperature of the meat:** In order for your meat to be done, it needs to hit a specific temperature. That temperature varies according to the type of meat. Chapter 3 has a table with the desired internal temperature for each type of meat.

There's a science to barbecue, and if you're willing to study and understand the time and temperature techniques, you can make great Q!

Starting with Great Ingredients

As with any cooking, the better the ingredients you start with, the better the resulting food. If you start with the cheapest cut of meat, chances are, you'll get just what you paid for. There are only so many ways that cooking can enhance meat. Try to start with the best meat you can afford.

Sourcing and choosing meat

When cooking great barbecue, start with a good cut of meat. You don't have to be rich, and you don't need a personal butcher. You *do* need to understand the basics of what you're looking for.

With some forms of barbecue, meat selection is everything. A prime example of this is beef. When cooking great beef barbecue, top grades are extremely important. Waygu or prime produce a seriously superior barbecue to lower-grade cuts. For beef, it's all about the marbling.

TIP

Any cut of pork generally has enough fat content to produce great barbecue. You don't need a super-premium, super-expensive cut. Pork butt — the typical barbecue cut — is very forgiving.

With any meat, ideally you want to find fresh cuts that haven't been frozen. If all you can find is frozen, make sure that it was flash frozen, which preserves the integrity of the meat. This is especially true for seafood — you don't want seafood that has any fishy smell to it.

TIP

You can source meat from a variety of places. If you have a great local butcher, see what she has available. If you don't have a butcher in your neighborhood, check your local grocery store. The big-box retailers typically have larger cuts of meat. Your local grocer typically cuts those large cuts of meat into smaller cuts that are more palatable to someone feeding a family of four.

To understand what to look for, head to Chapter 5, where I explain meat cuts complete with illustrations.

Keeping your spice shelf fresh

Spices are key to modern-day barbecue, but one thing is for sure: If your spices are old, they'll flatten or dull the flavor of your meat. Figure out what spices you use the most, and make sure that you always have them on hand, fresh. Spices typically have a shelf life of about a year when stored in a cool, dark place.

TIP

One way to keep your spices fresh is to use a table-top vacuum sealer after each use. If you have a vacuum sealer and good spice company in town, especially if you make your own rubs, look into buying the spices you use in bulk. This can save you both money and time, not to mention saving you multiple trips to the grocery store.

A great resource for spices in general and how to pair meats with spices is *The Flavor Bible,* by Karen Page and Andrew Dornenburg (Little, Brown and Company).

The book pairs different spices with different foods and vice versa. It's like a dictionary for spices. It includes the meats and other foods they complement.

Preparing the Meat

Certain pieces of meat are fine straight out of the package, but a brisket, for example, usually needs some trimming. In this section, I explain how to prep your meat before you cook it.

Trimming the fat

Most cuts of meat you find at a retail butcher counter are already trimmed so they have about ¼ inch of fat. However, if you buy a large cut of meat for barbecue, you may need to do some additional trimming.

Even ¼ inch of fat may be too much for your taste, so you may want to trim the meat down to the muscle structure of your meat. (Chapter 5 has information on trimming.)

Trimming can often enhance the flavor of your barbecue by making sure that your bark adheres to the meat without any waste. *Bark* is the outer crust of spices and fat that forms on meat as it cooks. It can sometimes make the meat look burnt, but bark is the essential element of flavor when barbecue is cooked properly.

TIP

A good, flexible boning knife is a must-have for trimming meat. A thin blade lets you get to the areas you want to trim and get right up against the edge of the muscle structure. (I talk about necessary — and unnecessary — tools in Chapter 3.)

Adding spices or liquid

Sometimes you just want the meat to stand on its own with no seasoning or alteration of the pure taste of the meat. However, more often than not, you want to add a bit of flavor or promote juiciness that you may not get with the plain cut of meat. Rubs, brines, and marinades are good ways to achieve an extra layer of flavor to take your dish over the top. Here's what each of these does:

>> **Rubs:** A *rub* is a mix of seasonings, sometimes including sugar, that you typically apply to the piece of meat right before throwing on the smoker. Some recipes call for the rub to be applied several hours in advance, but those are the exceptions.

Choose the rub you like for the cut of meat you're smoking and rub it in thoroughly by hand to ensure that the rub adheres to the raw surface of the meat.

TIP

Oftentimes in competition barbecue, pitmasters use plain yellow mustard as a base against the raw meat before applying the rub. The mustard helps the rub adhere to the meat. As the meat cooks, the mustard dissolves, essentially turning into vinegar while the rub sticks to the meat.

>> **Brines:** A saltwater-based brine penetrates below the surface and throughout the meat. You can inject seasoned salt water or submerse your meat in it for up to 24 hours.

>> **Marinades:** A marinade flavors the surface without penetrating too deeply. You typically place meat or vegetables in an oil-based seasoned bath for at least a couple of hours before you cook it.

Turn to Chapter 12 for recipes for rubs, brines, and marinades.

The Moment (or Hours) of Truth: Cooking

When you're ready to get going, make sure you take the steps to have a smooth and productive cook. The next sections tell you what those steps are.

Getting the grill or smoker ready

It may take a few hours to get your grill or smoker ready. Preheat your grill or smoker and get it up to the temperature that you need to cook.

Use a charcoal chimney or a wood- or paper-based fire starter to get your coals started. You can choose from several varieties of wood- and paraffin-based starters on the market.

WARNING

Avoid lighter fluid at all costs. You can find an easy way to get coals started without too much fuss and mess and avoid the off-putting odor and aftertaste that come with lighter fluid.

Make sure that the charcoal you use is high quality, clean, and dry. Charcoal that sits outside can get damp, and if it gets damp, it can gets moldy, which can affect the flavor of your cook.

Likewise, make sure that the wood you use to smoke is dry and handy so that you don't have to interrupt your cook to get more wood. Lay out the amount of wood you think you'll need to keep the smoke consistent throughout your cook.

Decide on your cooking method ahead of time:

>> **If you're cooking over indirect heat on a grill,** get the fire started at least half an hour to an hour before you want to start cooking. By starting early, you get a sense of how many coals to add at what intervals to keep your temperature consistent and even. You place the fire to one side of the grill and cook on the other side.

Figure out how you can add fuel to your fire without disrupting your cook. Some grills have a hinged grate that allows easy access to the coals in the grill. Others have a door to the fire box that you can open without disrupting the grate. If you have to lift the grate — and maybe your meat — to add fuel, just make sure that you plan for it ahead of time and have any tools you need close at hand to make it quick and seamless.

>> **If you're using a smoker,** get your fire started an hour or two before you put the meat on to cook. That way you heat up the outer walls of your smoker, which can seriously affect the time and temperature of your cook.

REMEMBER

Never underestimate how outside weather can affect your cook or the temperature of your smoker or grill. Smokers and grills with thin walls can be especially affected by the ambient air temperature, which can also greatly affect how that smoker or grill performs or how the temperature varies.

Altitude is another factor that can seriously affect the time of your cook, so if you're at a higher elevation than recipes are written for, take that into consideration. (All the recipes in this book were written for an elevation of 575 feet.)

Setting up for success

To set yourself up for success, plan out the elements you need to have a successful cook. Gather all the elements of your cook before you get started. Understand exactly what tools you need, what smoking method you're using, what meat you're cooking, the type of wood you're using, and how long you're cooking the meat.

There's nothing worse than being in the middle of a cook and realizing that you're missing a key ingredient or a key tool. Barbecue is about time and temperature, so the more prepared you are before you start, the more consistent your cook can be, and the better the results you end up with.

COOKING UNDER PRESSURE: COMPETING ON CHOPPED

In 2012, I was a contestant on the Food Network's cooking competition show *Chopped*. I remember it as invigorating, humbling, nerve-wracking, and fun. And I gained a healthy respect for the damage a simple shrimp head can do.

The format of *Chopped* is pretty simple and pretty tough: Four chefs are given a basket of mystery ingredients and 20 minutes to make a dish that incorporates all four ingredients. The baskets for my cohorts and me included tomatillos, *chayote* (a thin-skinned squash), Hawaiian blue prawns, and hatch-chile-flavored taffy. I had never seen or heard of chayote, so I tasted it. It's a bit bitter, a bit tart, and it has a pear-like consistency.

Now that I knew what I was dealing with, I set to work. I put four prawns on the grill, then headed to the well-stocked pantry to grab cornmeal, cream, butter, tarragon, and rum. I put the corn meal in boiling water to make grits and added cream, butter, and tarragon. In the meantime, my prawns had burned, so I had to start over. I pulled off the heads of four new ones, peeled and butterflied them, and put them on the smoker.

I threw the tomatillo and chayote into the food processor and pulsed a few times. It could be some sort of relish to go with the shrimp and grits, I thought. On to the taffy: My idea was to melt it down in the rum and use that as a glaze on the shrimp. I moved my grits and got the rum going. As I grabbed the taffy and threw it into the pan — whoosh! — the rum lit up in flames. I saw the camera guy come in for a close-up, so I tried not to act too surprised and like I meant for all this to happen. The taffy started to cook down and make a nice pink flambé.

I pulled the prawns off the smoker and put them on the grill. This time I watched them so they didn't burn. As I was getting ready to apply the taffy glaze, I decided that would take too long. So I put the glaze into the relish mixture in the food processor and pulsed one last time.

I wondered what exactly I'd made, when it dawned on me that it was a chow chow — a vegetable relish. I'm from Tennessee, so this was a Tennessee chow chow with low-country shrimp and grits.

With two and a half minutes left, I was golden. I just needed to plate the food, and I had plenty of time. I plated the grits, put a shrimp on top, and spooned on the chow chow. I felt great. And I had 30 seconds to spare, just enough time to add a garnish.

(continued)

(continued)

I'd seen shrimp heads with the tentacles waving on many fancy dishes. So, the four plates each got a shrimp head next to the grits. As the countdown ended, it struck me that nice, pink shrimp heads were one thing, and raw blue shrimp heads were not only unattractive but a health hazard.

So, yes, I was the first to go. The judges liked my dish but couldn't get past the food-safety issue posed by the raw shrimp heads. I didn't blame them. I hung my head and muttered "Bizzle Bap," my catchphrase. I was certainly disappointed but also glad that I'd at least finished in time. I made a bonehead mistake, but I presented a tasty dish. I'm glad I had the experience, but I probably won't look to repeat it anytime soon.

Chapter **2**

Uncovering the Science of Smoking

S cience? I thought we were smoking! I didn't know there was going to be science involved. Well, believe it or not, science plays a big part in any kind of cooking, including smoking meat. Reactions that happen at a molecular level determine when your meat is done cooking, whether it's tender, and how it tastes.

This chapter explains how your cooking methods affect the end result — your barbecue! I tell you when, why, and where to use these different methods.

Choosing Hot or Cold Smoking

You can choose from two methods of smoking:

» **Cold smoking** is the process of adding smoke while the meat remains cold and before it's cooked. You do this in a refrigerated cabinet or smoker that has a smoke generator added to it. Cold smoking uses a low temperature smoke source such as sawdust. This technique is commonly used on fish and sometimes bacon.

This method is typically used by an experienced chef or pit master. Cold smoking, if not done properly, can be dangerous. Cold smoking doesn't get meat hot enough to kill bacteria that can cause illness. If the meat is improperly handled or sits in the danger zone — 40 to 120 degrees — it can be a safe harbor for harmful bacteria.

Some foods are cooked after cold smoking, but sometimes cold-smoked food remains raw. If you're interested in this method, I recommend that you do more research and make sure that you fully understand the food safety measures you need to take.

>> **Hot smoking** is the process of not only smoking but cooking food with heat and smoke to get a finished, fully cooked product. Hot smoking is the more common method and the one I talk about exclusively in this book.

The process of hot smoking involves using an indirect heat source and burning charcoal or wood on the fire.

Burning wood is your best way to smoke. You add wood in the form of chips, chunks, or logs on a charcoal fire, a pure wood fire or, in the case of a gas grill, on a chip tray or smoke box. I talk about types of wood in the upcoming section "Some Words about Wood."

You can use wood chips and charcoal to maintain the correct temperature. Chips add more smoke, and you don't want to over-smoke, so use charcoal to maintain heat and chips or chunks to add flavor.

You need good combustion to make sure that the wood imparts a clean-burning smoke. To achieve this, you want your fire to burn close to 225 degrees. This temperature ensures that wood gets full combustion and allows your meat to cook slowly.

Knowing the temperature inside your cooker is key, so if your grill or smoker doesn't have a good thermometer, invest in one. You can find a good analog thermometer, or you can choose from one of the several digital models on the market. You can even get a wireless, remote thermometer.

How Meat Changes as It Cooks

As meat cooks, it changes physically. The heat changes the molecular structure of the meat. Also, certain chemicals in the smoke bind to the meat and change its properties, darkening it. Heat also alters water retention and allows oxygen to break free from the molecular structure of the meat.

Every time you penetrate your meat while it's cooking, heat pushes juices out of the holes you make, and that's not good. These juices ensure that your meat isn't dry or chalky.

TIP

Use tongs to turn meat rather than a fork — you don't want to puncture the meat and release the inner juices.

Don't flip too early; give the meat time to sear or seal up, typically five minutes or more depending on the cut. Burgers flipped too early, for example, start to fall apart. Searing and turning are all about cooking evenly and retaining moisture.

REMEMBER

When cooking large cuts of meat over low heat, the meat *stalls*, stops increasing in temperature, at 160 degrees. This is normal. The temperature may hold at 160 degrees for a few hours. Don't increase the temperature of your grill or smoker, just keep smoking. The stall isn't an issue with smaller cuts or items such as a steak that you cook hot and fast.

A successful cook — the right time, temperature, and amount of smoke — typically results in a nice pink smoke ring on the surface of the meat.

TECHNICAL
STUFF

A smoke ring forms when the collagen in the meat is affected by the nitric oxide, carbon monoxide, and oxygen produced during the smoking process. In other words, the smoke created has a chemical reaction with the outside of the meat to turn it pink and form the smoke ring. The ring doesn't penetrate deep into the meat because the gases can only penetrate so far.

The smoke ring is a preservative. Essentially, through a natural process, it cures the outside of the meat. A similar chemical reaction happens when you rub the meat with a curing agent such as a nitrate or nitrite as is done with pastrami, for example. Nitrates and nitrites are curing salts used to preserve meats like ham, salami, and bacon. They cause the same chemical reaction in meat that naturally occurs when smoking.

REMEMBER

Retaining the juices is the reason you let meat rest when it's finished cooking. *Resting*, which is just letting the meat sit at room temperature, gives the juices time to evenly distribute throughout the meat as it cools down. If you slice your meat before it rests, the juices ooze out and the meat loses that juiciness. When cooking smaller cuts such as a steak or burgers, turn the meat so that all sides get cooked evenly. When you flip, do so using tongs.

What to watch for when you're smoking

As wood burns, it puts off smoke. Having the right kind of smoke is critical. You don't want billowy smoke that pours from your cooker like water from a fire hose.

Look for a steady but not abundant amount of smoke exiting your smoker. You want an even, thin, light blue or white smoke, bordering on clear. That smoke comes from an even combustion burn. It's cleaner, with fewer impurities to taint your meat.

Black smoke coming from the smoker is not a good thing. If you have black smoke, carefully open the smoker just an inch or so a few times to let the smoke clear before you open the smoker completely.

WARNING

Don't open a smoker all the way when it's full of smoke. You can get a flashback that occurs when the smoke combusts. I've lost my eyebrows many times by forgetting to follow this warning.

At the end of your cook, your meat should have a nice golden or mahogany-colored look. When it gets to that color, stop adding wood to your smoker or grill. You don't want the meat to turn black or overly dark. If your meat starts to take on these properties, you have too much smoke. Stop adding wood to your fire.

TIP

When you smoke meat, look for a few key things:

>> **Understand the wood you're using.** Experiment with those woods to achieve the flavor you like. I talk about pairing wood and meat in the upcoming "Adding flavor with smoke" section.

>> **Make sure your wood is clean and dry.** You don't want a bunch of dirt on the wood, and moss or even mold on the outside can affect the flavor.

>> **Burn at a temperature that allow you to cook slowly but still get full combustion of your wood.** Aim for 225 degrees.

>> **Remember that too much smoke is a bad thing.** Don't smother your fire with too much wood. Give it enough to burn thoroughly.

>> **Keep in mind that smaller cuts of meat don't need to smoke for long.** Pork ribs, for example, cook in three to four hours. Don't over-smoke.

REMEMBER

You need to keep feeding the fire throughout the cook to maintain the right temperature, so keep your wood close (but not too close).

Cooking hot and fast or low and slow

Do you want to cook hot and fast or low and slow? Well, your cooking method depends on what you're cooking. Typically, the answer for barbecue is low and slow. Some chefs use a hot-and-fast method, but that's not the norm.

When cooking the larger cuts of meat typical for barbecue, the low-and-slow process helps the meat become tender by allowing the collagen strands to elongate and congeal. It also allows the saturated fats to break down and render, making the meat juicy. (Check out the next section "Muscling into structure and fibers.")

If you cook hot and fast, you risk those collagen strands bunching up and becoming tough.

Muscling into structure and fibers

When cooking barbecue, it helps to know about the structure of meat. The muscle tissue is what you think of as meat. But the structures you need to really understand are the collagen and the fat. The collagen and fat contribute a great deal to the flavor. In beef, the intramuscular fat contributes to the grading of the meat (see Chapter 5). The collagen is the connective tissue that holds the muscles together. I talk about each of them in the next sections.

TIP

Breaking down collagen and rendering the saturated fat in meats is the key to great barbecue. You often hear "low and slow" in cooking barbecue because that's the science of how your meat breaks down and actually becomes barbecue.

Cooking collagen slowly

Collagen is the protein in connective tissue. If not cooked properly, collagen bunches up and gets tough like a bundle of rubber. Cooking meat quickly guarantees it turns out tough.

Cooking collagen very slowly allows those fibrous strands to elongate, break apart, and let water in (in a process called *hydrolysis*). Slow cooking turns that collagen into a very soft, gelatinous substance that's tasty to eat and not tough at all.

Chewing the fat

Let's talk about fat. Animal proteins are high in saturated fats, or *triglycerides*. Those fats need to be broken down or elongated by cooking the meat very slowly. For barbecue, getting the meat to a high temperature — usually 192 degrees — is important for releasing the fat. At that temperature, the fat breaks down and renders or melts. Your barbecue will be done and very juicy.

Straight Talk about Indirect Cooking

When it comes to barbecue, you use two main cooking methods:

>> **Direct heat** is pretty straightforward: You cook the meat directly over the heat source. You do your everyday cooking on a stove over direct heat.

>> **Indirect heat** means that there are no coals directly underneath your meat. The heat source is separate from the cooking surface, but that heat flows to the meat and cooks it very slowly. There are many reasons to cook over indirect heat, but the science is in the temperature, airflow, wood, and how they all affect the meat.

Debating direct versus indirect

When do you use direct heat? Well, for grilling, you always want direct heat — it's the definition of grilling. Cooking over direct heat means the food cooks faster than with indirect. Direct heat also allows the meat to drip into the coals, and as that juice burns, it can add additional flavor to whatever you're cooking.

When do you use indirect heat? When you're smoking meats, indirect heat is usually the best method. By cooking with indirect heat, you can slowly bring your meat up to the proper temperature, and you have less chance of burning what you're cooking. You can use indirect heat with a grill, offset smoker, vertical smoker, or other cooking method (see Chapter 4).

REMEMBER

You can also use a combination of direct and indirect heat. For example, you can use the *reverse sear method* to cook a steak, cooking it on indirect heat for a bit and then finishing it on direct heat to sear the outside and seal in the juices.

Searing gives your meat a crispy, browned outer shell while simultaneously sealing in the juices. You can use two techniques to sear:

>> A **regular sear** involves placing the meat on a very hot surface to begin with and sealing all sides before you move it to a lower temperature to finish cooking.

>> A **reverse sear** is done near the end of the cook. You slow-cook the meat to 10 to 15 degrees below your desired final temperature; then you place it on a very, very hot surface — a grill or a hot cast-iron skillet, for example — to seal in the juices at the end.

Resting meat when it's done allows the juices to evenly distribute throughout the cut and provides an even, flavorful taste.

REMEMBER

Typically, you cook over direct heat when you grill and over indirect heat when you smoke barbecue.

TECHNICAL STUFF

Some types of barbecue use the direct cooking method. In North Carolina, for example, barbecue masters typically cook whole hogs over direct heat. They cook the hog slowly with the belly side, or open cavity, down and then flip the hog and cook the skin side. After flipping the hog, they crank the heat a little to crisp up the skin. The juices fall on the coals and as they burn, they add flavor to the meat. But cooking a whole hog isn't typical barbecue.

Making the most of the method

Which method — direct or indirect heat — do you use to cook your meat? Table 2-1 shows the best method for various types of meat.

TABLE 2-1

Preferred Cooking Method for Meats

Beef	Method
Brisket	Indirect
Burgers	Either, but mostly direct
New York strip	Direct
Rib roast	Indirect
Rib-eye	Direct
Short ribs	Indirect
Tri-tip	Either
Lamb	**Method**
Lamb ribs	Either
Shank	Indirect
Shoulder	Indirect
Whole lamb	Indirect

(continued)

TABLE 2-1 *(continued)*

Chicken	Method
Half chicken	Either
Leg quarters	Either
Whole chicken	Indirect
Wings	Either

Pork	Method
Butt	Indirect
Pork belly	Indirect
Pork chop	Direct
Pork loin	Indirect
Ribs	Either
Shoulder	Indirect
Whole hog	Either

Some Words about Wood

Wood plays an important role in barbecue. In fact, wood is the essential ingredient. Cooking barbecue means smoking meat with wood, chips, chunks, or logs. You can use whatever type of smoker or grill you want, but if you aren't smoking with wood, you aren't making traditional American barbecue.

Wood for barbecue comes in a range of sizes, shapes, and levels of dryness. The sizes and shapes range from small pellets to large logs:

>> **Pellets:** Specifically designed to be used in pellet smokers, pellets are actually compressed sawdust and very efficient in the smokers they're designed to be used in. Pellets aren't just your smoking tool on these cookers; they're also the primary heat source.

   Pellets come in all different flavors, which is nice because you can create a blend of flavors with varying amounts of different types of pellets.

>> **Chips:** Chips for smoking are typically about 1-inch square. They burn faster than larger pieces, so use them accordingly and sprinkle a few chips at a time. Some people soak their chips in water for a longer, more sustained burn.

Chips typically come in a bag about the size of a plastic grocery bag and are available at most hardware, home improvement, and sporting goods stores throughout the grilling season.

The nice thing about wood chips is that you can blend several different types to get a desired flavor. For example, mesquite and apple is a great combination for a smoked prime rib.

>> **Chunks:** Chunks are typically about 4 inches in size and provide a long-burning, yet compact way to add smoke to your fire. If you want something that burns longer than chips, but you don't have the room for logs, chunks are your solution. Using chunks means you don't have to babysit your fire as much.

Chunks are effective for offset smokers and certain vertical smokers. You can also mix and match them for different flavors.

Chunks are available at most hardware, home improvement, and sporting goods stores throughout the grilling season.

>> **Logs:** Logs are the purest form of wood for burning in a smoker. Typically about 12 to 18 inches in length, they come in various thicknesses and are usually split. Logs are the longest-burning type of fuel and give you the most flavor.

REMEMBER

Logs are for bigger smokers. You want the size to match the size of your smoker. Obviously, a smoker with a big firebox can take bigger logs than one with a small firebox. Trial and error can show what size is best for your smoker.

Most of the time you need to get logs from a firewood supplier. Most areas have specialty wood businesses.

TIP

Store your wood in a cool, dry space. As wood gets older, it *seasons*, or dries out, which makes it burn faster. Most chunks and chips are kiln dried so they're already pretty dry.

Your grill or smoker determines how you use wood and what type of wood you use:

>> With an **offset smoker,** it's pretty clear that you throw the wood in the firebox and let 'er rip.

>> A **vertical smoker** doesn't have as much room for wood as an offset, so you use chunks or chips. Load them in combination with charcoal throughout the cook, and you should be okay.

>> On a **gas grill or smoker,** you use a *smoking tray,* a non-combustible device with holes in it to allow the wood to burn and release smoke without fouling up the grates on your gas grill.

Chapter 4 elaborates on grills and smokers.

In addition to the varieties of wood you can use, various stages of wood seasoning (drier versus wetter) affect the way it cooks and flavors the meat. With wetter wood, you get a longer burn and more smoke. This is great when your fire is going strong and the coals are hot enough to burn through that wood. If you want to get your heat up and raise the temperature of your pit, drier wood works best.

TIP

For a hot fire, use dry wood. For more smoke, use a wetter wood that will smolder.

Flavoring as You Smoke

You can flavor your meat before, during, and after you cook it. I talk about seasonings and sauces you typically apply after the cook in Chapters 6 and 7. The next sections, however, give you pointers on applying flavors before you smoke and on using the smoke itself to add flavor.

Adding flavor with smoke

Smoke brings flavor to the barbecue party. Smoke imparts the flavor of the wood along with moisture to the cooked meat. The best way to do this is with natural wood or charcoal. Different woods impart different flavors to the meat you cook over them. Some woods pair better with certain types of meat than others (see Table 2-2).

WARNING

Smoke carries flavor but can also carry a bitter, acrid taste, so you don't want to overdo it. Too much smoke can also discolor your meat. Smoke is like any other ingredient: You want to use it in moderation.

It's difficult to over-smoke large cuts of meat, so you're pretty safe there, but you can easily over-smoke smaller cuts like ribs. For smaller cuts, use a dry, seasoned wood that burns fast and with less smoke than wet wood.

TIP

To prevent over-smoking ribs or smaller cuts, cut down the cook time and use a little higher heat — 250 to 275 degrees for ribs.

Table 2-2 offers suggestions for which type of wood works with specific meats.

Testing the effects of brines and rubs

Brines and rubs can have a tremendous effect on the meats you cook. Some people like to brine, some rub, and some do both. Many barbecue competitors use both methods with great precision to achieve the taste desired by the judges. (Chapter 6 has lots of information on brines and rubs.)

TABLE 2-2

Meat/Wood Pairings

Meat	Wood Recommendations
Beef rib	Mesquite, oak
Brisket	Mesquite, oak
Chicken	Hickory, oak, pecan
Fish	Alder, maple
Lamb	Fruitwoods, mesquite
Pork loin	Fruitwoods, hickory
Pork shoulder	Hickory, oak, pecan
Pork tenderloin	Fruitwoods, hickory
Steak	Mesquite, oak, pecan
Turkey	Hickory, oak, pecan

REMEMBER

When you brine or rub, remember that you're altering the natural flavor of the meat. Depending on the taste you're trying to achieve, that can be a good thing or a bad thing.

Adding salt water

Brining is the act of injecting a liquid into a cut of meat to impart flavor. You can also brine by submerging a piece of meat in a liquid.

TIP

Many people don't understand how to brine or the science behind it. If you remember your science teacher talking about osmosis, you'll understand how a brine works. The key to brining is using a saltwater base so that the flavor penetrates the cell wall structure and carries it throughout the molecular structure of the meat. As the sodium binds to the protein, it allows the meat to pull in more water and, thus, become moister.

Some brines contain sugar or flavor enhancers as well as salt water.

Hams are brined with a sodium nitrate that keeps the meat pink. Many of the meats you buy in the grocery store are brined. The meat industry has used brining techniques for years to produce juicier, weightier, and more flavorful cuts of meat.

TIP

Before you start to brine on your own, make sure that your piece of meat hasn't already been brined. If the package says "15 percent solution added," that means that the meat has been subjected to a sodium or sodium-and-phosphate brine. (Phosphates help meat retain moisture and, thus, weigh more.)

Rubbing on flavor

Adding a rub is done just like it sounds: You rub a seasoning mix on the meat. Most people sprinkle it on and then rub it in. Others like to use plain, yellow mustard as a base coat before applying a rub; the mustard helps the rub stick to the meat and dissipates as the meat cooks, leaving little to no additional flavor.

When it comes to rubs, the first thing to know is that there's a difference between a rub and a barbecue seasoning:

>> A **rub** typically has a high salt or sugar content. You use a rub on meat before it's cooked to alter the flavor of the meat in some way.

>> A **barbecue seasoning** doesn't necessarily alter the flavor of the meat itself; you add a seasoning *after* the meat is cooked. (The famous Peg Leg Porker Dry Rub falls into this category.)

   You cook dry ribs with little to no seasoning. You put them over the wood of your choice and then hit them with the seasoning right before they hit the plate. This allows the fullness and brightness of the spices to come through as a seasoning on the naturally smoked meat.

The base for rubs can vary greatly. Many rub recipes start with chili powder or paprika. They may have a good bit of salt or sugar depending on the flavor profile you want to achieve. Many competition cooks look for a sweet heat, so you see some sugar in the rub and possibly cayenne or another chili to heat it up a bit. (I share some great rub recipes in Chapter 12.)

Steak rubs are more for when you want to grill, but even if you want to smoke a steak and add a rub after, you can't beat a simple rub with rosemary, thyme, salt, and pepper. Those four seasonings are a good rub for many types of meat.

Sometimes simpler is better. For example, in Texas, many people use only a salt-and-pepper rub with brisket and beef ribs. It's a very effective seasoning, and it helps cut through the fat on a large piece of meat like a brisket.

Finally, in many areas, cooks don't use a rub at all — they just sprinkle the meat with salt and start smoking. This is the most natural way to cook a meat like pork because salt enhances the flavor but doesn't mask it. Often, when using this method, you baste the meat while it cooks with a vinegar-based *mop* (a liquid seasoning blend used to keep your meat moist). I cover sauces in Chapter 13.

Chapter **3**

Stocking Up on Barbecue Tools

You can find a lot of barbecue tools — not just smokers and grills, which I describe in Chapter 4, but an endless amount of accessories. You can spend $20 or $20,000 depending on your level of commitment. What do you really need? Well, you can get by with the basics. When you spend more money, you get more. The choice is up to you (or your wallet!).

In this chapter, I walk you through various options at all levels of the spectrum — from backyard barbecue to the pro circuit.

Starting a Fire

You can try many ways to light your smoker or grill and find a number of tools to help you do it including the following:

>> **A charcoal chimney (see Figure 3-1):** Old trusty has been a staple for backyard cookers and pros for decades. (Your grandfather probably made one from an empty coffee can, back in the day when coffee came in large cans.) A charcoal chimney is a metal tube 8 to 10 inches in diameter, about 18 inches high. It has

a mesh grate about 4 inches up the tube and a handle. You add charcoal in the top part and newspaper in the bottom; then you light the newspaper to ignite the charcoal above it. It's a very clean and efficient way to start charcoal.

FIGURE 3-1:
A charcoal
chimney.

Photograph by Quinlan Ulysses

TIP

A charcoal chimney is clean, easy to use, and dependable as the day is long. If you don't have one, get one. All you need to get your coals going in no time is a chimney, charcoal, a match, and some newspaper. You don't need starter fluid of any type, so your coals burn very cleanly.

>> **A propane weed burner (see Figure 3-2):** One of my favorite ways to get my fire going is with a propane weed burner. This is essentially a large propane torch or flame thrower. You can pay about $40 for one at a home improvement store.

WARNING

Make sure that you have somewhere to set this tool after you light your fire because the head of the torch gets very hot. Also steer clear of the gas hose so you don't accidentally burn a hole in it. You need to take care with this tool, but it can start your fire in about three minutes and is fun to use as well.

>> **An electric flame starter (see Figure 3-3):** Similar to a weed burner, an electric flame starter is more compact than a weed burner and plugs in. It is effective and safe, and it starts a clean-burning fire.

Photograph by Quinlan Ulysses

FIGURE 3-2:
A propane weed
burner.

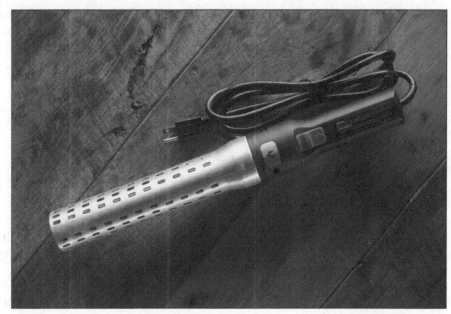

Photograph by Quinlan Ulysses

FIGURE 3-3:
An electric
flame starter.

>> **Fire starter:** You can find various fire starters on the market, such as Royal Oak Tumbleweeds (www.royaloak.com/products/tumbleweeds-firestarters). They're easy to use, compact, and get your fire going. Most are a combination of paraffin and some form of accelerant. Some are all natural, containing just sawdust and paraffin, others may leave a little lighter-fluid taste.

However you start your fire, avoid lighter fluid. It can leave a chemical residue on your meats.

REMEMBER

A Mop, Some Tongs, and More

The right tools and accessories can make your cooking life easier, safer, more comfortable, and even more fun.

The following sections talk about the must-haves and the nice-to-haves.

The essentials

Your kitchen may already be stocked with many of the tools of a good barbecue cook. If you don't have any of the items in the following list, think about adding them as you embark on your barbecue career:

>> A covered baking dish or two

>> Nonreactive bowls (glass or plastic)

>> Hot gloves or oven mitts

>> A large sheet tray

>> A good, large stock pot (12 to 20 quarts)

>> Mixing spatulas

You need some protective gear when you cook barbecue. You'll need fire-safe shoes or boots (no sandals allowed), as well as an apron. The apron saves your clothes; the shoes save your toes from stray coals.

You may already have some of the other essential tools listed here; if you don't, add them to your barbecue supplies.

>> **Silicone basting brush:** If you want to be able to slather your meats with a sauce or baste — and, trust me, you do — having a silicone basting brush is

essential. Before silicone became more prevalent in cooking, these brushes were more like paint brushes with natural bristles. The new and improved silicone brushes are just as effective and more sanitary to wash and reuse.

>> **Cast-iron skillet:** A cast-iron skillet is a kitchen staple. It has various uses and is great on the grill.

>> **Good gloves:** You'll need a variety of pairs of gloves when you're working with barbecue:

- *Black latex or nitrile:* These are great for handling raw foods and help you keep a food-safe environment. You can find them at most stores.

- *Woven cotton gloves and latex gloves:* When your barbecue is cooked, you need gloves to handle it. I like to use a woven cotton glove with a latex glove over it for this task. This combo insulates you from the heat and allows you to handle the meat out of the smoker. Because the combination isn't very thick, you still have the dexterity you need.

- *Elbow-length, high-heat gloves:* If you're pulling meat off the smoker, you may also want some elbow-length, high-heat gloves. You can still use the cotton under them for insulation but elbow-length gloves are a little stiffer than the cotton with latex, so you won't be as dexterous.

TIP

- *Welding gloves:* With the protection of welding gloves, you can handle a hot charcoal chimney or a firebox. They're fairly inexpensive to buy and are likely to become one of your top tools.

>> **A good knife:** For trimming your barbecue, you need a good, sharp knife. I like a boning knife or filet knife because they're thin, flexible, and easy to handle.

>> **A barbecue mop:** This tool is literally a little mop for your meats — like a miniature version of the old-fashioned mop you might mop your floors with. It typically has a 12- to 18-inch wooden handle with a cotton rag mop head — I like a long handle, myself. A mop allows you to baste during your cook and finish with sauce if you like.

Mops are great because they're disposable and fairly cheap, and they get the job done.

TIP

Some people like a silicone mop for finishing, but silicone is fairly useless with a thin basting sauce. A cotton rag mop works with either thick or thin sauces, so that's what I recommend.

>> **A good thermometer:** You need a precise indicator of when your meat is done. Many people go by feel, which is great for a seasoned pro, but you can't beat knowing exactly where your meat temperature is when you want to get it right. I prefer a quick-read digital thermometer. Tell-Tru (www.teltru.com) and ThermoWorks (www.thermoworks.com) both make excellent products.

A remote temperature probe is also great to use. You can choose one of many on the market, some with Bluetooth capability and apps that let you track your cook all the way through.

You can find a good thermometer online or at a cooking supply store.

>> **Tongs:** You can find good, commercial spring-loaded tongs at most restaurant supply stores. You may want to have more than one pair. I like to have a couple of lengths on hand: 8 inches up to 14 inches.

REMEMBER

If you're using a gas or electric grill, you need a smoke box to hold wood chips or chunks that add flavor to the meat. I talk about flavoring techniques in Chapter 2.

Nice but not necessary

Some tools aren't really necessary, but they can make the job easier. I include nonessentials in the following list:

>> **Butcher paper:** Use butcher paper to wrap meat while it cooks over indirect heat or after it cooks, while it rests. You don't always need it, but it can come in very handy.

>> **Draft fan/temperature control unit:** This device takes an internal pit temperature and feeds oxygen to your fire to keep it at the temperature you set. Some also have a meat probe to monitor your cook and back the heat off when the meat is close to done. This tool revolutionized backyard smoking and has helped many barbecue enthusiasts cook better barbecue.

A draft fan isn't cheap, but it gives you the freedom to remotely monitor the temperature of your cooker and your meat and makes your life much easier. Most manufacturers make adapters to fit all kinds of cookers. One example is the BBQ Guru Pit Viper 10 CFM Fan (https://bbqguru.com).

>> **Dutch oven:** This large cast-iron pot and lid are great for making stews and other liquid dishes. You can put it directly in the coals, which makes it very handy.

>> **Grill basket/grill screen:** Made with finer mesh than a barbecue grate, a basket or screen helps you cook vegetables and other smaller foods on the grill without having them fall through the grate.

>> **Spray bottle:** Helpful in spritzing your meat to keep it moist, you can fill a spray bottle with water, juice, vinegar, a mop sauce, a baste — or a combination.

As you grow into your barbecue-chef self, some of these tools may move to your personal essentials list.

Chapter **4**

Looking at Smokers

For most home cooks, what, how, and where you cook are the high-ranking motivations for any smoker purchase. If you're a whole-hog kind of cook with a huge patio, you won't opt for the same smoker as a brisket enthusiast with a tiny deck. Even within those categories, there's a dizzying array of options spanning fuel source, material, and, of course, cost.

You wouldn't buy a Jet Ski to travel the Sahara, and you don't want to drop a lot of cash on a commercial offset smoker if all you're ever going to smoke is a chicken or two at a go. You can do that with the kettle grill you inherited from Dad.

Then again, equipment is fun! And I'm certainly not above getting a charge from eying the latest, greatest, most powerful cookers on the market. To help you approach the big decision, in this chapter I give you details about various types of smokers and why you would, theoretically, choose each.

The question you need to ask yourself is how big of a commitment you're willing to make to barbecue and what that looks like. Do you want to smoke like a pro on a professional rig, or do you just want to cook for your family and have something versatile and suitable for various types of cooking? This chapter covers all your options.

Getting by with a Grill

You can smoke barbecue with a typical, backyard grill. If you're just starting out, this option isn't a bad way to go because you have a tool (your grill) that lets you

>> Cook with direct heat directly over the fire.

>> Cook with indirect heat by placing what you're cooking to the side of the fire.

>> Sear meat on a very hot grate.

>> Cook low and slow to smoke barbecue.

Any grill with a lid, such as the kettle grill shown in Figure 4-1, can become a smoker when you keep your heat source on one side and your food on the other. Some accessories make this easier. Several tools hold coals to one side of a charcoal grill or create a heat barrier while letting the smoke come through. A barrier like this is fine if you aren't cooking a lot of meat or a really large cut of meat.

FIGURE 4-1:
A kettle grill becomes a smoker when you push the heat source to one side.

Photograph courtesy of Carey Bringle

Whether you like a standard kettle grill, an adjustable-grate grill, or even a propane model, relying on a grill can be a good starting point to smoking.

TIP

When smoking on a regular grill, your ability to control the heat is limited. A grill with adjustable grates helps you gain some control and is a nice feature whether you're grilling or smoking. If your fire is too hot, move the grates farther from the meat. If it isn't hot enough, move your protein closer. It's that simple.

REMEMBER

The finish on your grill can be important. Most grills come with a high-heat painted steel finish. That's fine. But if you don't cover your grill, this material will rust through. Stainless steel is a great finish and should last years, but it's more costly and it can be hard to keep clean if you don't keep it covered.

One newcomer to the market is the recently revived PK Grill. Made from cast aluminum, it's an excellent choice for a grill. These light and versatile grills were used by troops on the front lines of the Vietnam War. They have a fixed cooking area and fire grates and an elongated shape, which is very helpful when you're using them to smoke. The surface area is fairly hardy, too, so you can use them for many applications. You can find out more about PK Grills at www.pkgrills.com.

Do you want a gas grill or a charcoal grill? The answer may depend on where you live. If you want the most authentic type of cooking, charcoal is the way to go. But gas may be your best option in certain circumstances. Both types have pros and cons, which I run through in the following sections.

REMEMBER

The choice between gas and charcoal is a personal one. Don't let anyone tell you you're cheating with gas. Many people don't live where they can have an all-wood cooker. For some people, gas may be the only choice. No biggie. We all deserve good barbecue. Be like a Marine: Adapt and adjust. There's more than one way to smoke a brisket.

Considering charcoal

You get the most authentic barbecue flavor with a charcoal grill. The live coals and smoke from both the coals and the chips or chunks of wood you can add get you what you're looking for as far as taste.

Plus, you don't need the extras when you use a charcoal grill and a good hardwood charcoal. The charcoal imparts the flavor you want to your meat. You can always add more wood or chips or chunks, but a good hardwood charcoal comes standard with good flavor.

Charcoal grills are both affordable and accessible to most everyone; Figure 4-2 shows a typical grill. Charcoal itself is readily available.

On the downside, you have to watch the grill closely to monitor the temperature and add fuel. Cleanup is no picnic, either (excuse the pun).

FIGURE 4-2:
A typical
charcoal grill.

Photograph by Quinlan Ulysses

Overall, you get a great experience with charcoal.

TIP

A helpful feature to look for on a charcoal grill is a hinged grate or a fuel door to make adding fuel easier.

Grilling with gas

If you want something faster than a solid-fuel grill, you can go gas. The number of gas grills on the market is astonishing, with prices ranging from $100 to a head-spinning $10,000 — you can really go high end.

TIP

I say find a good stainless-steel gas grill on wheels for portability. The same rules apply as for any grill: Find something sturdy and reliable.

With a gas grill, such as the one shown in Figure 4-3, you have the benefit of a constant temperature and regulated fuel supply. When you find the right setting for your burners, you can walk away with the confidence that your temperature will remain consistent.

FIGURE 4-3:
A gas grill.

Photograph by Quinlan Ulysses

You can smoke with a gas grill — you just need something to hold the wood chips or chunks over the gas burner without fouling it up. You can use a cast-iron skillet or a stainless-steel smoke box like the one shown in Figure 4-4. You can even wrap some wood chips in aluminum foil. The key is that you have something that holds the chips or chunks over the flames so they smolder but don't fall into your gas burners.

A nice feature of a gas grill is the ability to tap into your house's gas source with a flexible gas hose. This helps you avoid having to go refill propane tanks every weekend. However, if you connect to your gas line, you may need a natural gas conversion kit. Natural gas has a lower pressure point than propane.

Time, temperature, and smoke are all elements of good barbecue, and you can achieve all these in a gas smoker if you set it up right.

FIGURE 4-4:
Use a smoke box
to add flavor
when cooking on
a gas grill.

Photograph by Quinlan Ulysses

Leveling Up: Considering Smokers

So, you've moved past the grill and you want to move up to a dedicated smoker. This section explores the issues to consider. What you purchase may affect how you feel about smokers for a long time to come.

Why buy a smoker? Well, there are many reasons. A dedicated smoker allows you to fully focus on the art of smoking. It allows you to hone some skills that may be useful when you move up to the big leagues of smoking.

Buy a smoker because you love to smoke great food or because you want to work on perfecting the craft of smoked meats.

TIP

You can get smokers in all different types, sizes, and shapes, but you may want to start off small to get the feel of your particular barbecue style.

The more you get into smoking, the more you realize that you want a consistent temperature throughout the smoker. As you progress in your particular style, you get to know what you want and you can tune your cooking to the particular setup you're cooking on. Be patient!

What are your options for smoking? The next sections talk about the basic types.

Standing up to a vertical smoker

A *vertical smoker* is an upright cooker with the firebox on the bottom and the cooking chamber directly above it (see Figure 4-5). The upright configuration utilizes the natural tendency of heat to rise with the heat source on the bottom and cooking surface on top, making it very efficient.

FIGURE 4-5:
A vertical smoker.

A vertical smoker is a good beginner option, and it's readily available. You can choose from charcoal versions, gas versions, and electric versions of vertical smokers.

Vertical smokers are great for smaller cuts of meat because they have tall, thin chambers; however, some great professional verticals can handle much larger cuts, including a whole hog. They have a small footprint and typically give you a good amount of cooking space.

REMEMBER

The bottom line on a vertical smoker is that it takes up a small amount of space and is usually very efficient, which makes it a great choice for a backyard enthusiast.

Vertical smokers can get much hotter up top. Just like horizontal smokers, they need to be tuned to make sure that the heat is as even as you can get it. Higher-end, more expensive verticals are tuned, whereas cheaper models are just letting the heat rise in a natural manner and make no effort to eliminate hot spots.

Some vertical smokers on the market are really just a smoker with a fire pan on the bottom; the meat hangs above a fire in the bottom or sits on grates above a fire. The heat rises, so you have a very efficient smoker. Other verticals have a baffle system so the meat isn't directly above the flames of the firebox.

In a baffled vertical smoker, a dampening system keeps the fire from coming into direct contact with the meat. That system may be a plate that's slightly smaller than the body of the cooker, so it allows the heat to rise up and around the perimeter of the plate, or it may be a water pan, which also adds moisture to the meat while cooking.

Some cooks like to fill the water pan with something other than water to bring a specific flavor to the meat as it cooks. You can use orange juice, apple juice, vinegar and water — the sky's the limit. Whatever you choose, make sure that you keep an eye on the liquid level. You don't want it to evaporate and leave you with a burnt pan.

WARNING

If you use a water pan in your smoker, make sure that you're truly smoking low and slow (see Chapter 1 for reasons why). If you cook at too high a temperature with a water-pan smoker, you end up steaming your meat rather than smoking it, which isn't what you want.

Just as in a horizontal smoker, a vertical can be reverse flow to promote better circulation. In this case, air usually travels between an inner and outer wall and is dumped on the top of the cooking chamber. The air is then forced down to vents in the bottom back wall of the cooking chamber that then exhausts the smoke. This method provides a more even temperature throughout the entire chamber.

Table 4-1 lists pros and cons of various vertical smokers.

TABLE 4-1   **Vertical Smokers: Pros and Cons**

Type	Example	Pros	Cons
Top feeding	Weber Smokey Mountain Cooker Smoker Pit Barrel	Efficient Very affordable	Reloading charcoal can be frustrating May have to move meat to reload fuel
Front feeding	Masterbuilt	Easy to load and maintain Firebox door opens separately from the chamber door No heat loss with refueling	Can have big temperature differences between the top and the bottom

Siding with an offset smoker

An *offset smoker* smokes food in a chamber separate from the heat source, which is in a different chamber attached on one side. The smoker usually has a horizontal body where you place the meat; the wood or charcoal burns in the firebox to the side of that chamber (see Figure 4-6). Heat flows through the body of the smoker and out the chimney on the other side.

FIGURE 4-6:
An offset smoker.

Photograph courtesy of Lang BBQ Smokers

The *firebox* is the chamber where wood or charcoal burns. It has a large door for feeding the wood or charcoal in and vents that allow you to adjust the airflow. The fuel sits on a grate at the bottom of the firebox, which allows it to burn cleanly and vent properly.

Offset smokers have been around for a long time. They're the most common and abundant type of smoker on the market for the general public. They're very versatile and fairly straightforward to use. And it doesn't hurt that they're easy to come by — most companies make some sort of offset smoker. You can find one for $100 or $1,000, depending on what you want to spend.

TIP

As an amateur smoker, you won't go wrong with an offset smoker. It gives you lots of room for larger cuts of meat and helps you get familiar with the basics of smoking and airflow. When you get better at smoking (and can justify spending more) and understand how your vents work to control airflow, you may consider a more sophisticated offset with a baffle system or a reverse flow.

Offset smokers are preferred in Texas because they're great air movers and provide a perfect vessel for smoking brisket or beef ribs — products that really need swift airflow to get the best results. (Chapter 2 has more detail about how smoking works, including tips for matching meat to method.)

Are offset smokers a lot of work? Well, they can be. The cheaper models are loosely built, and heat may not flow as well as it does in a more expensive model. The key is making sure you have a good thermometer placed well, which means about 3 inches up from the grate and somewhere on the unit where it won't hit the meat you're cooking.

REMEMBER

Regardless of the cooker you use, maintaining an even temperature throughout is important. Even heat is exactly what a smoker with baffles or reverse flow offers you. These features are typically found on bigger units more suitable for an intermediate cook. You may want to cut your teeth on a smaller, cheaper offset to start.

In a standard offset, the area by the firebox that's the source of your heat gets very hot. In order to lessen this effect or get a more even heat flow, some offsets use *tuning plates* (rectangular steel plates situated under the grates). You use them to regulate the heat flow up through the body of the cooker. The plates are placed more closely together closest to the firebox and farther apart as distance from the firebox increases.

Stacking with a vertical offset

A vertical offset smoker functions like its horizontal counterpart but with an up-and-down body. Its vertical chamber is especially accommodating for meats like sausage or ham that need to hang. Figure 4-7 shows a vertical offset smoker.

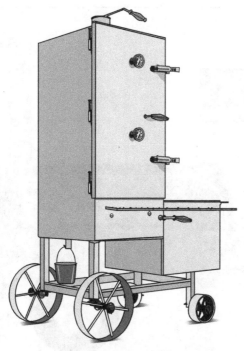

FIGURE 4-7:
A vertical offset
smoker.

Vertical smokers have great airflow and really move the smoke through the chamber. Because heat rises, it hits every area of the hanging meat, which gives you a fairly even cook. Although it's hotter at the top, the heat envelops the meat on its way up the chamber.

The fact that the heat rises through the smoking chamber makes a vertical smoker quite efficient. Plus, it has a smaller footprint than a horizontal one. The limiting factor of a vertical offset is that it can't hold larger cuts like a whole hog.

REMEMBER

You have to feed your vertical smoker frequently, which means you can't step away from your smoker for very long. Even though some have insulated fireboxes, they still need to be fed wood or charcoal about every 45 minutes to an hour.

Making a U-turn with a reverse-flow offset

A *reverse-flow offset* moves air from the firebox across the body of the smoker and back again to a chimney next to the firebox (see Figure 4-8).

Lang BBQ Smokers®
Original Reverse-Flow
Design Since 1988

FIGURE 4-8:
A reverse-flow
offset smoker.

**TECHNICAL
STUFF**

A reverse-flow offset is similar to a regular offset smoker with the exception of the airflow inside the smoker. Typically in a reverse-flow offset, a plate below the grate forces the air to flow down the smoker. At the far end of the smoker (opposite the firebox) is a gap that allows the air to flow upward. The chimney is placed on the side of the smoker, where the firebox resides, so the air then flows back down the smoker to exit out of the chimney. Basically, the heat flows down the smoker, does a U-turn, and then goes back out the chimney.

Reverse-flow offsets have a solid *baffle* (a panel for redirecting heat) under the grate that takes the heat all the way to the other end of the cooker. Because the chimney is built into the smoker on the firebox side, air has to travel all the way down the smoker and back to the firebox side.

MAKING YOUR OWN SMOKER

Offset smokers are easy to make. Many people use an old propane tank or a large steel pipe. (Just be sure to safely ensure no propane is left in the tank.) The key to a great offset horizontal smoker is getting the air to flow evenly.

You can find many resources out there for making your own smoker. There's no point in looking, though, unless you're a competent welder or you have a friend who is. You don't have to be the best, but a basic ability to draw a bead is necessary. If you don't know what that means, leave the welding to someone else.

Aaron Franklin has some videos on building a horizontal offset smoker, so you can check that out and get the scoop (www.pbs.org/video/bbq-franklin-episode-4-pits). And I've posted a few how-to videos myself (www.youtube.com/user/PegLegPorker/videos). Or just hit YouTube, type in "how to build a smoker," and be prepared to be amazed at how many people have videos walking you through the process.

Building a smoker is a commitment. Even if you know what you're doing, you need some serious time. Getting it right takes a while. Be patient and know that what you build, if taken care of, can last a generation.

Relying on electric pits for renegade smoking

This is the smoker that gets all the dirty looks — it's the bad boy of the barbecue world. *Electric smokers* heat the cooking chamber and create smoke by drawing electricity rather than relying on fire. They produce a consistent result but are considered cheating by many barbecue enthusiasts. To these minds, no fire means no true barbecue.

But electric pits do have value for many applications. Large smoking operations often use electric smokers to produce deli meats, hams, and other processed meats. Large electric smokehouses often are used in conjunction with electric hot plates that heat and smolder sawdust for smoke.

Residential electric smokers like the one shown in Figure 4-9 usually are vertical smokers about the size of a dorm fridge with an electric element in the bottom. The element heats the chamber, and the chips or pucks of wood smolder to produce smoke.

FIGURE 4-9:
A residential electric pit can be an effective way to cook meat evenly — especially for beginners.

Electric smokers don't really cook very differently from traditional smokers except for the fact that they use an electric element as a heat source. You need to add some form of smoke, typically wood chips or sawdust, to get the desired smoking effect. You can run an electric smoker without wood chips or sawdust, but then you're cooking the way you would in an oven.

TIP

When looking into electric smokers, pay attention to what type of smoke source they use. Some have proprietary wood pucks, and some use common wood chips. I lean toward something that doesn't use a proprietary smoke source. That way, you have much greater flexibility in the type of smoke source you use — and where you find it.

Barbecue is about time and temperature. Electric smokers can provide both very efficiently. They're very precise, which allows you to produce a consistent product.

Many of the newer electric smokers on the market have timers and even Wi-Fi controls. They have become quite sophisticated and allow even an amateur to produce quality barbecue with very little knowledge. Don't be intimidated by the haters. If you're a beginner, this may be the pit for you.

TECHNICAL
STUFF

Most electric smokers in the commercial world are large smokehouses with roll-in racks. Not seen often by the general public, they're probably the way the majority of commercial smoked meats are created around the world. The precision and consistency of electric smokers make them ideal for large commercial use.

Spinning through rotisserie basics

A *rotisserie smoker* includes a mechanism that spins the meat as it cooks so that all sides are exposed to the heat source and, thus, cook evenly. Rotisseries come in all shapes and sizes; Figure 4-10 shows a common example.

FIGURE 4-10:
You find a wide range of rotisserie configurations; as long as the meat can spin, you get the even cooking you're looking for.

Photograph courtesy of Ole Hickory Pits

Typically, the carousel that holds the meat is a spindle with shelves hanging from various points. Most configurations have four or five hanging points with three shelves per hanger. They load efficiently because you can rotate the racks to you, and they tend to have a large capacity due to the nature of the configuration. Rotisseries are great for cuts like ribs, chicken, butts, and brisket.

I love rotisseries because they get consistent temperature, airflow, and circulation, which means that no piece of meat is sitting in an area with low air flow.

Gas-assist rotisseries are the most common. These smokers burn large wood logs and use gas to assist in the cook when needed. The process is pretty simple:

1. **Load the firebox chamber with wood.**

2. **Set the temperature.**

   The gas blower lights the wood. After it's started and up to the temperature you set, the gas stops and lets the wood do the work. If the fire drops below the desired temperature, the gas comes on again to get the cooker back up to temp. The gas assists the wood for a consistent temperature, but the wood does most of the heavy lifting.

3. **Load your meat.**

4. **Add wood throughout the cook.**

J&R makes several all-wood-fired rotisserie smokers (www.jrmanufacturing. com). They use baffles and vents to adjust the temperature based on what you set, but they have no gas or electric assist.

Electric rotisseries, which have an electric heating element and burn chips or sawdust, used to be more common, but you really don't see them much anymore. They just aren't as efficient as fire is for cooking barbecue.

If a barbecue restaurant does a good bit of volume, chances are, they use a gas-assisted rotisserie. Gas-assisted rotisseries are consistent, and they allow you to set a temperature and walk away for an extended period of time. There has always been a fierce debate on whether this is cheating in the barbecue world. I can tell you that, in many cases, a rotisserie is the safest, most efficient way for a restaurant to get consistently good results with its barbecue.

Adding pellet smokers: A trend for good reason

The latest rage in smoking is *pellet smokers,* which rely on compressed wood dust, or *pellets,* to provide fuel. They're pretty impressive. The pellets are very compact and burn very efficiently. Figure 4-11 shows a standard pellet smoker.

TECHNICAL STUFF

The same pellets that power these smokers used to be a fuel for home furnaces. Somewhere along the way, someone thought that they would use them in smokers and grills. What a good idea!

FIGURE 4-11:
Pellet smokers
offer a satisfying
mix of real wood
smoke and
technology that
ensures an even
temperature.

Photograph courtesy of Green Mountain Grills

To use a pellet smoker, you set the temperature, and a battery- or electric-powered corkscrew mechanism feeds enough fuel to the fire to get to that temperature without feeding it too much. When the cooker reaches your desired temperature, the corkscrew stops feeding fuel.

REMEMBER

Pellet smokers have the same benefits as electric smokers, but they burn wood with no need for an electrical element. The fuel makes for a very efficient burn and consistent temperature.

You can choose from different types of hardwood pellets or use a blend. Because the pellets are very compact, you don't need tons of space for a woodpile.

TIP

If you like the convenience of an electric cooker but the flavor of all wood, a pellet smoker is the way to go.

When shopping for a pellet smoker, make sure you consider the capacity of the hopper: How many pellets does it hold and how long will it be until you need to add more to keep it going? Look also at the cooking space. If you're planning to cook a lot of turkeys, for instance, you need to make sure you can accommodate a big bird.

A modern pellet smoker may include digital controls and Bluetooth and/or Wi-Fi. You get accurate temperature control without being chained to your smoker and can even check and adjust your temperature remotely — pretty convenient. This connectivity makes pellet smokers a great choice for the "set it and forget it" cook. Of course, more complex controls mean you spend more money.

Joining the cult of ceramic cookers

Often touted as smokers, *ceramic cookers* rely on natural-lump charcoal for fuel and dampers for temperature regulation. They are amazing at holding temperature and can go from 300 degrees to 1,200 degrees in a matter of minutes. Figure 4-12 shows the most popular ceramic cooker, the Big Green Egg.

FIGURE 4-12: Based on tandoori ovens, ceramic cookers like the Big Green Egg enable quick temperature adjustments.

Photograph courtesy of Carey Bringle

A ceramic cooker is really a *tandoori*, or Indian oven. Ceramic cookers gained popularity in the United States when Big Green Egg (https://biggreenegg.com) introduced them. Now they have an almost cult-like following. Eggheads, as they call themselves, are devoted to ceramic cookers and are fiercely loyal to their brand.

You can add wood chunks or wood chips when using a ceramic cooker, but your primary fuel is natural-lump charcoal.

You adjust the temperature by opening dampers at the bottom of the unit and in the top of the lid. Doing so increases or decreases airflow and oxygen to the fire, precisely regulating temperature. By using the dampers, you can adjust the temperature up or down in a matter of minutes.

WARNING

Before you raise the lid during a cook, you need to *burp* the cooker — that is, open it about an inch a few times before opening it fully. If you don't burp your cooker, the smoke can ignite to create a massive fireball and give you quite the burn.

Ceramic cookers are great for barbecue because of their precise temperature control. Their efficiency enables you to smoke at a constant temperature for an extended period of time without having to reload the fuel, which is great for cooking things like steak. You can cook your steak at 350 degrees, remove it from the heat, increase the airflow, and then sear at a very high heat. This process is called a *reverse sear,* and it makes for quite the tasty meal. Chapter 2 tells you more about cooking methods.

TIP

You can choose from many different brands of ceramic cookers on the market today. Look for quality ceramics and make sure you buy one that has a ceramic interior. Some may look like ceramic, but they're just insulated metal walls. If you want to get fancy, you can find elaborate versions with tiled exteriors, which may add to the looks but doesn't affect how they cook.

Building an open pit smoker

The first type of smoker I used to cook for a group of people was simply cinder blocks, some tin, and a hole in the ground. It was crude, and it wasn't easy to regulate, but my homemade pit got the job done. You can improve on my method and build your own direct-fire barbecue pit, which should look something like Figure 4-13.

Gather some simple materials:

>> A shovel

>> 54 cinder blocks

>> 4 pieces of rebar or steel rod 40 inches long

>> A 40-x-56-inch piece of ½-inch plywood

>> A 30-x-46-inch metal grate

>> Heavy-duty aluminum foil

© John Wiley & Sons, Inc.

FIGURE 4-13:
A cinderblock
pit with a
roasting hog.

Choose relatively level ground about 4 x 6 feet in area with no overhanging trees. Clear the grass or other vegetation before you get started. To build your smoking pit, follow these steps:

1. **Shovel out a 4-x-6-foot patch of ground about 1 inch deep.**

   You can leave the bare dirt or fill the area with sand to help insulate the pit.

2. **Line up the blocks for the first course:**

   a. Set three blocks on the first short side.

   b. Starting at the outside of the end row, lay four blocks on the long sides.

   c. On the other short side, set a block on each side, leaving a gap in the middle.

3. **Lay the second and third courses, staggering the cinderblocks.**

4. **Place four pieces of rebar or heavy-gauge steel bars about 1 foot apart across the width of the pit.**

   You may need to notch out some blocks so that the rebar stays level. The steel rods form the base for the cooking grate.

5. Lay the last course of cinderblocks.

6. Place a 30-x-46-inch metal grate on the rebar stretchers.

7. Wrap a 40-x-56-inch piece of ½-inch plywood with heavy-duty aluminum foil to serve as a lid.

    You can also make a lid from a large piece of tin.

TIP

An 80-x-46-inch piece of chicken wire folded in half can make a kind of taco shell for the hog. Encasing the hog in chicken wire helps hold it down and helps you flip it.

To keep an eye on the temperature, place an oven thermometer in each corner of the pit.

TIP

Coat the face of a thermometer with cooking oil before placing it in a fire pit. When the thermometer smokes up, you can wipe the face to clear away the smoke and read the temperature.

Buying a Cooker: What to Look For

Cookers come in all ranges, shapes, sizes, and qualities. Even if you're just starting out, look for a good-quality smoker or grill so that you can become a good-quality cook. A cheap cooker will just frustrate you.

WARNING

A low-quality smoker won't give you consistent heat, which is key to great barbecue. Choose a smoker that you can count on.

A couple of points to consider when you're looking to buy a grill or smoker:

» **The size of the cooking area:** The more cooking area the better. Get as large a cooking area as you can afford or have the space to house. A big cooking area lets you cook a greater quantity of delicious barbecue, and it allows you to get your fire farther away from the meat you're smoking. The ability to have a fire on one side and meat on the other is a great benefit.

» **Price:** Get a cooker you can afford. Smoking is no fun if you're so broke you can't afford to buy the meat to cook on it. You don't want to be scrambling to pay for supplies because you spent too much on your grill.

    Set a budget and stick with it. If you do your research ahead of time, this shouldn't be a problem. You don't want to be grill poor.

When you first start smoking, you may not mind loading more fuel into your smoker every 30 minutes, but as you mature in your cooking, you'll start valuing efficiency. You want a smoker that keeps consistent heat over a long period of time. So, buy a quality smoker that will keep you happily smoking for a long time.

The qualities to consider as you shop for a smoker or grill that affect cooking include the following:

>> **Reliable airflow options:** In other words, good vents. You want the vents to be tight, and you want the right amount for the size of the grill, meaning vents on the bottom and the top.

Make sure the vents move smoothly and open fully to provide proper airflow. Read reviews to make sure that the grill or smoker you choose doesn't have a problem getting up to temperature. Typically that indicates a vent or airflow issue.

REMEMBER

Having the right airflow and the ability to regulate that airflow is critical. Being able to regulate airflow gives you the ability to regulate temperature, which is key.

>> **An appropriate footprint:** Make sure the smoker or grill fits where you want to keep it.

>> **Even heat distribution:** Not easy to see from a visual inspection, you need to go online and read some reviews. Do your research to make sure that the cooker performs well.

>> **The material and construction:** Grills come in all different materials:

- Painted steel is the most common material, which is fine. Just remember to cover it up to protect the finish. When a grill starts to rust, it can deterio-rate very quickly.

- Stainless-steel grills are great for durability and they stand up to the elements better than painted steel.

- Cast-aluminum grills are durable and lightweight. They hold up to the elements and are fairly well insulated.

WARNING

You don't want to load a rickety grill with hot coals. It's dangerous and could end up hurting you or burning something down.

The construction of a grill or smoker is a key consideration. You want a well-assembled, well-put-together smoker. Look at the following:

- *The thickness of the steel:* The thicker the walls are or the thicker the steel is, the more heat retention you get. Heat loss through thin metal walls can be a problem, especially in the winter.

  Keep in mind that a cooker that uses thick steel has substantial weight.

REMEMBER

- *The amount and type of insulation:* More insulation is better, and grills that come insulated typically have the appropriately rated insulation.

  If you buy a smoker from a custom maker, make sure that he or she understands what the proper insulation is. Stay away from any insulation not specifically rated for heat.

- *How tight the welds are:* Look at the welds and make sure there are no gaps. Gaps let heat and smoke out. Some products are *tack welded,* meaning just certain spots are welded instead of the whole seam. You want to stay away from tack welding and look for a smoker with continuous welds along the seams.

- *The weight and thickness of the grates:* Grates can be made out of a number of metals, but their weight is important. You don't want thin metal strips that will rust or a flimsy wire grate that will deteriorate quickly. A stainless-steel grate or cast iron is ideal. Carbon-steel grates are fine, but you need to season them like a cast-iron skillet.

  Any metal grate that isn't stainless steel can and will rust eventually.

>> **A good thermometer or the ability to add one:** You want to be able to change out the thermometer on a grill or smoker, so look for a smoker that has a threaded thermometer. This feature enables you to change out the thermometer if it goes bad or upgrade to a more reliable thermometer if needed.

WARNING

Be prepared! If you cook enough, you will eventually have a fire — see the nearby sidebar, "From bar fridge to smoker to molten puddle" for my personal experience. If you have a grease fire in a steel cooker, it won't necessarily ruin the cooker if the steel is thick enough. If you have a grease fire in a thin-walled cooker, you can cause real damage and get badly burned.

FROM BAR FRIDGE TO SMOKER TO MOLTEN PUDDLE

It was Thursday, and some of my barbecue teammates and I were where we always were on Thursdays — our regular bar. Out back sat an old fridge that gave us ideas. We struck a deal with the owner: For 40 bucks we'd haul it away. We took it to my house and began to break it down. Luckily, it had regular batting fiberglass insulation, which came out completely. If you get a fridge that has foam in place of insulation, run — the foam is highly toxic.

We replaced the fiberglass batting with rock wool insulation and put it back together. We added a firebox. It was no easy task because the exterior of the fridge-turned-cooker was aluminum. It had to be tungsten inert gas (TIG) welded. It was a great cooker, but it would've been much better had it been stainless steel.

One day, I was cooking on it in my driveway. I put too many logs in the firebox and then walked away for an extended period of time, leaving the firebox door open. I came back to a raging inferno. I hadn't cleaned the cooker in a while, so there was an excessive amount of grease in the bottom of the cooker body. When I saw the firebox raging, my first inclination was to close the door. Bad idea. The fire jumped from the firebox to the body and hit that grease. It caught fire immediately and blew both doors open. I had a full-on grease fire. That fire proceeded to melt the aluminum body to the ground.

Lesson learned. Build your cooker out of materials that can take the heat.

2

Knowing the Ingredients for Success

Look into meat, the basic barbecue ingredient. Check out the primals — the basic cuts — of beef, chicken, lamb, and pork. And get to know the person who supplies your meat — your butcher can be your best barbecue bud.

Add flavor before you cook with rubs, brines, and marinades. Develop some precook flavor habits. Rub on spices or soak meat in a marinade or brine to preseason your meats.

Get saucy after the cook. Although not all barbecue traditions involve sauce, many do, so test various types to discover what sauce you like with which meat.

Chapter **5**

Starting with the Meat

Sure, I guess you can barbecue vegetables, but meat — almost any kind of meat — is what barbecue is made for. This chapter tells you how to find the meat to smoke, talks about methods, and explains the best cuts to use.

Making Friends with a Butcher and Other Ways to Start Strong

It used to be that the best way to get cuts of meat was to make friends with your local butcher. That's not as common anymore because local butchers aren't nearly as common as they used to be.

TIP

Wherever you shop for meat, make sure the selection is good and the meat looks fresh.

Searching for your butcher

Traditionally, butcher shops just cut meat from *boxed meat* (commercial cuts from big packing companies). However, a new breed of artisan butcher is out there. Nowadays, butchers are much more likely to process their own beef and to work closely with local farmers to source great meat.

The artisan butchers of today are very aware of where their meat comes from, how the animals were raised, and what new cuts are available. If you can find an artisan butcher, that's great; if not, there are plenty of options online or you may find a local grocery store with a great meat counter.

REMEMBER

You can find a butcher at your local grocery's meat counter, a dedicated butcher shop, or your local farmers' market. No matter where he works, a good butcher is

>> Willing to custom-cut your meat to a desired thickness or specification

>> Able to fully explain the cuts to you and let you know what the cut is recommended for

>> Knowledgeable about the origin of the meat

When you find a butcher you like, build a relationship that will serve you both for years to come.

Being knowledgeable about meat

Sometimes all you need to shop for meat is some common sense. Beef should have a bright red or pink appearance, for example. With beef and pork, you want to see marbled fat, which gives the meat flavor.

During the '80s and '90s, when the government guidelines declared a low-fat diet the healthiest, pork producers tried hard to compete with the lean meat of chicken. (Remember the slogan, "The other white meat"?) This resulted in pork that was almost devoid of marbling or fat — and flavor. Luckily, nowadays, heritage breeders have popped up and you can find well-marbled pork cuts with a good flavor and texture.

When shopping for chicken, look for birds raised without hormones. Poultry breeders are happy to brag about their best practices. If you can find pasture-raised birds from a local farm, buy them. They have a better taste than commercially raised chicken. It's hard to make chicken taste bad, but starting with a quality bird will up your barbecue game.

When looking for fish, get the freshest you can find. You never want a fishy smell or any sort of slimy feeling. Fresh fish has a firm texture and little to no smell.

Knowing Butt from Belly: Cuts of Meat

Knowing about the cuts of meat can help you choose one to smoke today. (Tomorrow, you can choose a different meat and a different method.)

TECHNICAL STUFF

In talking about meat cuts, it makes sense to start with the *primals,* the large hunks cut off of the carcass. The primals are then broken down into smaller retail cuts of meat for steaks or for grilling and smoking.

The next sections run through the types of meat and the cuts that make for the best barbecue.

Smoking beef

When people talk about cuts of meat for barbecue, they mainly talk about beef brisket and beef ribs, the two most common cuts.

The U.S. Department of Agriculture (USDA) assigns grades based on several factors:

» **Marbling:** The intramuscular fat throughout the muscle of the meat. Marbling is a factor in how beef is graded. Lots of marbling is what you're looking for.

» **Maturity:** The physical characteristics of the meat. It's almost impossible to tell how old a beef cow is, so USDA graders look at certain characteristics of a carcass such as bone characteristics, color, and texture to assign a grade.

» **Quality:** The quality of the cow. The quality of the cow is judged by an inspection of the carcass. Factors an inspector looks at include marbling, firmness of the meat, and color of the lean and fat of the meat.

Beef grades according to the USDA, starting from the top grade, are

» Waygu, or Kobe beef

» Prime

» Choice

» Select

» Standard

- » Commercial
- » Utility
- » Cutter
- » Canner

TIP

The best cut of beef, waygu, is not easy to find and is very expensive; if you can find it and afford it, it provides the best end product. Prime is easier to come by and is generally available from a good butcher. If you live someplace where the local grocery store is your meat market, choice may be the best grade you can find. Select doesn't have enough marbling for good brisket or short ribs. Think of select as about the cheapest steak you buy. Anything below the select grade — standard through canner — won't work for you. They're typically commercial cuts that aren't suitable for the barbecue you want to make.

Figure 5-1 shows the eight primal cuts of beef on a steer. Starting at the front is the chuck, or the upper part of the animal, next to the neck and shoulder. Behind the chuck is the rib, followed by the loin. The round is the back part of the cow. Underneath that is the flank, and moving toward the front are the short plate, the shank, and the brisket.

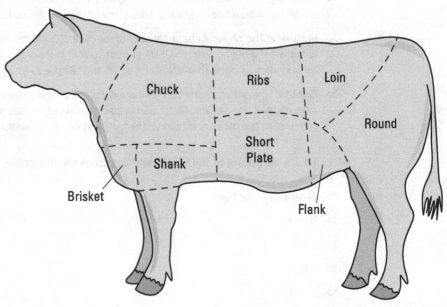

© John Wiley & Sons, Inc.

FIGURE 5-1:
Basic, or primal,
beef cuts.

Some primals are used for barbecue, including the brisket and the prime rib. However, for grilling, you typically use a lower-grade piece.

Many retail cuts of meat can come from the eight primal cuts identified in Figure 5-1. In fact, you can get approximately 74 retail cuts. I won't go through all those in this chapter, but I talk about some of the most common retail cuts you can use for grilling or for barbecue in the following sections.

Brisket

Brisket is typical Texas barbecue. It's the cut that really defines what Texas barbecue is all about. Brisket is also one of the most common cuts of meat cooked on an offset smoker with post oak or mesquite. (I talk about grills, smokers, and fuel in Chapter 4.)

Brisket comes from right under the chuck on the breast of the cow right next to the shank (refer to Figure 5-1). A brisket is made up of two parts:

>> **Flat:** The flat is the thin part of the brisket and the leanest section of the meat.

>> **Point:** The point, sometimes referred to as the *deckle,* is the fat end of the brisket and has a layer of fat running right through the middle of it.

If your brisket is very thin and flat, it's more than likely a flat cut with the deckle, or point, removed. The flat is a very lean cut of brisket, which makes it difficult to retain moisture and flavor when you cook it. I suggest cooking an entire brisket with both the flat and deckle intact. This way, you get a lean section of meat on the flat and a fatty section of meat with a lot of flavor with the point.

TIP

Before cooking a brisket, be sure to trim it. A good rule is to leave about ¼ inch of fat on the brisket. This gives you consistent rendering of the fat when you cook and insures that you have a nice layer of *bark* (the beautiful crust on the outside of the brisket when it's fully smoked) with your fat and rub.

Trimming fat may seem counterintuitive with brisket because fat equals flavor, but trimming takes away only the outside fat — you aren't removing fat from the inside of the meat, which is where the flavor comes from. By trimming, and leaving just ¼ inch, you allow enough fat for flavor but keep it thin enough so that the bark doesn't slide off when you slice the meat. Having the bark stay on each slice ensures flavor in every bite.

REMEMBER

With a brisket, the quality of the cut, or the grade of meat, significantly impacts the quality of the barbecue you produce. With pork, just about any pork butt will do and make great barbecue, but with brisket, the higher the grade, the higher the quality of the barbecue.

Beef ribs

Ribs are also a straight-up Texas dish. Smoked beef ribs are known as a world-class delicacy made famous by cooks such as Louie Mueller in Taylor, Texas.

A cow has 13 ribs, starting at the front of the cow and moving back toward the short plate (refer to Figure 5-1).

You can get two types of beef ribs:

>> **Beef back ribs:** These are attached to the rib-eye cut of meat.

>> **Short plate or short ribs:** These are lower than the back ribs on the cow and extend down toward the belly next to the brisket.

Beef short ribs are typically 5 to 6 inches long, whereas a beef back rib is typically between 8 and 12 inches long. Both can have a significant amount of meat depending on how the butcher cut them or how they were separated from the rib roast.

The most common style of Texas barbecue for beef ribs is a beef short rib; although they're called a short rib, the ribs can weigh about a pound apiece. Short ribs are a whale of a meal to smoke, but they're mighty good when done right. Beef ribs, like brisket, are typically cooked in an offset smoker with post oak or mesquite. That's Texas style. (I talk about smoking in Chapter 2.)

As with brisket, the grade of the meat for the beef ribs determines the texture and tenderness of your barbecue product after it's smoked, so buy the best cut you can afford.

Grilling cuts of beef

In talking about steak for grilling, the most common cuts are New York strip, T-bone, porterhouse, tenderloin, rib-eye, and sirloin.

New York strip

I start with my favorite cut, the New York strip. The New York strip, or strip steak, is cut off of the short loin primal (refer to Figure 5-1). This steak has robust flavor and is typically a little chewier than other cuts.

TIP

If you can find a good marbled prime New York strip, there's no better steak on the cow. It's a steak lover's steak. The New York strip is also part of the T-bone or porterhouse.

T-bone and porterhouse

Some people think that a T-bone and porterhouse are the same cut, but they're not. Both are cut off of the short loin, so they come from the same primal, but what makes a porterhouse a porterhouse instead of a T-bone is the distance from the bone to the edge of the tenderloin on the tenderloin side of the steak. A T-bone or porterhouse is composed of both a New York strip and part of the tenderloin. So, you get two steaks and two great flavors and textures in one big steak.

TECHNICAL STUFF

In order to be considered a porterhouse and not just a T-bone, the steak must have 1½ inches from the edge of the bone to the outer edge of the tenderloin side of the steak. So, a porterhouse has more meat on the tenderloin side than a T-bone does. The porterhouse is cut on the thicker end of the short loin; the T-bone is cut off of the thinner end of the short loin. Both have great flavor — one just has more meat.

Tenderloin

The tenderloin comes high off of the back of the cow from the short loin primal. It's the area of the cow's body that gets the least amount of exercise, making the meat extremely tender. Tenderloin steaks, otherwise known as filet mignon, are considered to be the caviar of beef. Typically the most expensive cut, tenderloins tend to be a little bit leaner than a New York strip or rib-eye, but they can have great flavor, and they're very easy to eat.

Rib-eye

Rib-eye comes off of the rib primal. The rib-eye is typically richly marbled and has a fat eye right in the center of the steak. You can get it either bone-in or boneless. I recommend boneless rib-eye because it's easier to cook and takes up less space on your grill. Use bone-in rib-eyes when you want to make a big impression with the look of your steak.

Rib-eye is a very flavorful steak that actually has two different textures:

>> The main body of the steak, what some called the *princess cut* of the rib-eye, has a nice texture similar to a New York strip but is a little more tender and generally more marbled.

>> The top of the rib-eye, or the *cap,* is actually a muscle called the spinalis. The *spinalis* is the top muscle or piece of meat above the round eye of fat in the middle of a rib roast. It has a grainier, bloodier texture and different flavor than the rest of the roast. Sometimes the spinalis is cut off the top of the rib-eye and served as *top-cut rib-eye.* The whole rib-eye with the spinalis in place is a very flavorful steak.

A cut that's very popular today is the *cowboy-cut rib-eye*, which is a rib-eye steak with a full rib bone intact. The bone gives the steak added flavor, and it's quite an impressive-looking cut of meat.

Sirloin

The sirloin comes from the sirloin primal. It's boneless and is typically a little chewier or meatier than most other steak cuts. Sirloin is a cheaper cut, but it has gained popularity in recent years with large restaurant chains able to offer it at a reasonable price. The sirloin, if prepared correctly, can have great flavor and texture.

TIP

I suggest using a tenderizer and good seasoning with sirloin.

Cutting up chicken

Where I come from, we call chickens "yardbirds." Whatever you call them, they can make some great barbecue.

A chicken consists of six primals, as shown in Figure 5-2:

>> Neck

>> Back

>> Wing

>> Breast

>> Leg

>> Thigh

One chicken can yield as many as 18 retail cuts. Chicken cuts for barbecue are typically the following:

>> **Whole bird:** Whole bird is just that — the entire bird, gutted and with the giblets and neck removed. Whole birds are ideal for smoking because you can stuff them, and they tend to retain a great deal of moisture.

>> **Half a chicken:** Half a chicken is ideal for barbecue because it gives you both kinds of meat (white and dark), retains its moisture, and has a skin that gets crispy as it cooks.

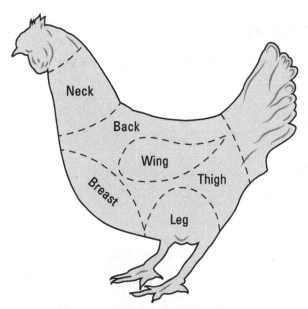

FIGURE 5-2:
Cuts of a chicken.

© John Wiley & Sons, Inc.

In the south, half a chicken is a typical barbecue dinner. The half chicken is big enough to give you get four cuts from the bird — breast, wing, thigh, and drumstick.

» **Leg quarters:** Leg quarters are a very economical choice. Legs and thighs are usually the cheapest cut of meat, and they're juicy and flavorful. Backyard grilling wouldn't be complete without leg quarters.

» **Wings:** Wings are great for smoking or fast grilling. In the past, people threw them away, but wings have now become a staple in the American barbecue diet. Wings are generally readily available at your local grocery store. They can be prepared a variety of ways. (Look for my wings recipe in Chapter 9.)

All chicken cuts are delicious when cooked correctly.

WARNING

Many people choose boneless breasts when they grill. They're not my favorite because it's very difficult to keep them from overcooking. Most people tend to dry out breasts on the smoker or grill. The thigh is a juicier cut that's easier to maintain over fire.

Looking at lamb

The lamb has four major primals, shown in Figure 5-3:

>> Leg

>> Loin

>> Flank

>> Front

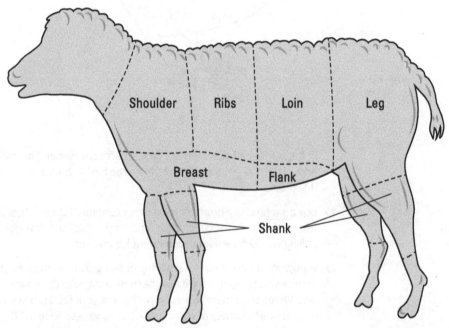

FIGURE 5-3:
Lamb primals.

© John Wiley & Sons, Inc.

From those cuts come some 13 cuts of retail or restaurant cuts of meat. The cuts most used for barbecue are

>> **Rack of lamb:** The rack of lamb is cut off of the lamb loin (refer to Figure 5-3). This cut usually has six bones and is great for smoking or grilling. Rack of lamb is a great cut of meat, tender and flavorful.

>> **Leg of lamb:** The leg of lamb is just that, the leg primal, and it's great for smoking. This particular cut is most like a pork shoulder and can be smoked to be pulled just like pork. The lamb shoulder can be cooked the same way. This is a popular dish in Kentucky, where it's called mutton.

>> **Lamb ribs:** Lamb ribs have become quite popular in recent years. Although they don't have a lot of meat, they can make a very flavorful rib. I've seen them in Texas and Tennessee.

Portioning pork

You can buy a lot of different cuts of retail pork, and many of them are great for barbecue.

Breaking down a hog starts with the four main primals:

>> Shoulder

>> Loin

>> Belly

>> Leg or ham

Figure 5-4 shows the pork primals and some good barbecue cuts.

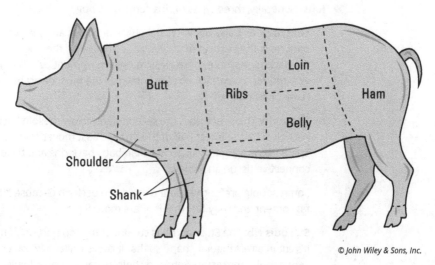

© *John Wiley & Sons, Inc.*

From the four primals, a hog breaks down into more than 22 retail cuts. Here are the ones best for barbecue:

>> **Whole pork shoulder:** Whole pork shoulder is traditional barbecue that's a staple in the states of Georgia, Kentucky, North Carolina, Tennessee, and Virginia. Pork shoulder produces pulled pork, chopped pork, and sliced pork. A large cut of meat that typically weighs between 10 and 17 pounds, pork shoulder lends itself to great pulled pork.

Probably the most prominent pork cut you've heard of for barbecue is pork shoulder. The shoulder consists of a shank and the butt. It's essentially the whole, front leg with the shank and shoulder bones intact.

>> **Butt:** The butt (sometimes called *Boston butt*) is actually the top portion of the shoulder minus the shank and the shank bone. This cut of meat is typically in the 5- to 9-pound range. A butt has less waste than a whole pork shoulder due to not having the shank.

TIP

Butts are sold two ways, bone-in and boneless. I recommend bone-in butts. They have more flavor and tend to loosen up more when cooking, which makes them generally more tender. The main way to cook a butt is a bone-in, whole butt.

>> **Ribs:** Generally, three types of ribs come off a hog:

 • **Loin back or baby back:** The loin back or what's also known as the baby back rib is the best cut of rib. It comes highest off the hog, so it's closer to the backbone where there's less muscle movement, which makes the meat very tender. Baby back ribs are known as the most desirable or most tender ribs on the hog.

 • **Spare rib:** The spare rib is the section right below the loin back or baby back ribs. It's the lower half of the rib cage as it moves toward the belly. Spare ribs are a much larger cut than baby back ribs and have much more connective tissue and sinew.

 Some people prefer the spare rib to a loin back rib because it has a higher fat content and they feel that it offers more flavor.

 • **St. Louis rib:** The St. Louis rib is cut out of the top portion of the spare rib. It's cut in a rectangular shape so that it cooks uniformly, which makes it very popular for restaurants and chefs. Because the St. Louis rib is part of the spare rib, it has great flavor and texture due to its high fat content and connective tissue.

>> **Belly:** The belly on a hog is just that — the stomach. Bellies are cured and then smoked to make bacon. Belly meat is very high in fat content and is very well marbled, making it one of the most tender and desirable meats on the hog. In addition to being used for bacon, the belly is used a lot in Asian cuisine and also used in very high-end restaurant recipes.

>> **Leg or ham:** The leg, or the *ham,* is a great meat for the smoker. You can cook a ham barbecue style to produce pulled pork. Hams can be cured and then smoked to make what's commonly known as deli ham. When meat is cured and dry smoked or aged, it's called a traditional country ham, or prosciutto in Italy.

>> **Pork chops:** Pork chops come off of the loin. Chops can be smoked like barbecue, but they're traditionally grilled.

>> **Pork loin:** The pork loin comes off the rib and is typically boneless. Pork loin can be smoked whole. Traditionally, it's cut into chops and grilled.

>> **Crown roast:** A crown roast is a pork loin with the ribs still attached. It's often served at a banquet or a nice dinner with the ribs tied in a circle for dramatic effect.

Savoring seafood

You can choose from many types of seafood to make good barbecue. Probably the most common is salmon. It has a bold flavor and takes smoke very well. Smoked or grilled salmon is delicious. (Check out Chapter 9 for a recipe.)

Other abundant and delicious fish to smoke are trout and catfish. They are both widely available, take smoke well, and are delicious.

Lastly when it comes to fish, consider shellfish. Lobster or crab can be great with a little smoke, but shrimp and oysters really shine. Smoked or grilled oysters are always a treat and safer than raw. Shrimp is easy and quick to cook on your smoker or grill.

Chapter **6**

Preparing the Meat: Rubs, Brines, and Marinades

I n this chapter, I talk about the whys and hows of preparing your meat before you put it in the smoker. Whether you decide to use a rub, a brine, or a marinade depends on what you're trying to cook and what results you're trying to achieve.

TIP

Check Chapter 12 for recipes for all types of meat preparations.

Prepping Meat for Heat

As you get ready to cook, one of the decisions you need to make is how you want your meal to taste. Seasoning, brining, and marinating can all change the flavor of the meat. Some people like just salt and pepper, others like sweet, and others like heat. You can achieve whatever results you want through your meat preparation. In the following sections, I talk about the different ways to prepare your meat and how each affects what you're cooking.

Previewing the preparations

One part of a successful smoke is the heat, another part is the meat, and another part is how you prep and treat the meat. You virtually never put a plain piece of meat on the grill. What you do beforehand plays a large part in how the meat tastes when you're done cooking it.

The following list explains the common pre-cooking procedures:

>> **Brine:** A liquid — typically, a salt-and-water combination — that you immerse meat in before cooking to promote juicy tenderness.

The standard ratio is 1 cup of salt to 1 gallon of water. You fully immerse the meat in the brine and put the container in the refrigerator for at least four to six hours. Rinse the meat when you take it out of the brine before you start smoking it.

REMEMBER

Typically, you cook brined meat right away. If you let meat sit in salt water too long, it begins to cure.

You can also inject brine using a very large syringe, a method I discuss in the upcoming "The juice on brining" section.

>> **Marinade:** A liquid mix that you soak raw food in before cooking. Marinades generally contain an acid such as vinegar or wine and/or oil along with spices.

Marinades, unlike brines, typically don't penetrate the whole muscle of the meat; instead, they flavor the outer surface. You want to achieve full contact, so go full immersion or place the meat or vegetable in a bag with the marinade.

You typically marinate food for two to three hours, but you can marinate overnight for deeper flavor penetration.

>> **Rub:** A mix of seasonings applied to the surface of the meat. You can put a rub on right before cooking or, for deeper penetration, several hours before you cook. Rubs are meant to alter the outer layer of your meat.

Planning reactions

Salt, acid, fat, and heat all affect the flavor, texture, and consistency of your meat. Each one contributes in its own unique and special way:

>> **Salt:** Simply put, salt enhances flavor. It's the most basic form of seasoning, but the most important. Discovering how and when to use salt can be the difference between being a good cook and a great one. However, salt is an

ingredient just like any other and can be used too much or too little. Start with a little and add as you need to. **_Remember:_** You can always add more salt, but it's very hard to take it away. Large cuts of meat can take much more salt that small cuts.

>> **Acid:** Acid balances flavor. Fat and salt can both be enhanced or balanced out with a touch of acid. The acidity that lemon juice, vinegar, lime juice, or any other type of acid adds to a meal can balance flavor between the salt and the fat.

>> **Fat:** Fat carries flavor. Typically, when you're cooking barbecue, the fat is already on the meat and you don't need to add it. In recipes that call for fat, such as beans, you can use fatty meat like bacon or lard.

>> **Heat:** Heat transforms your meat. Whether you cook hot and fast or low and slow is the determining factor in how your barbecue turns out. In barbecue, the heat is almost always low and slow. You're typically dealing with fatty cuts of meat that need the time and correct temperature to properly break down.

Barbecue is all about temperature and time, which means low and slow.

REMEMBER

The mixture of acid and fat almost always insure great barbecue; it's a combination made in heaven. Because barbecue meat tends to be very fatty, the acid can really cut through that fat and balance out the flavor. In the Carolinas, the acid comes in the form of a vinegar sauce, which is typically mixed in with the meat from a whole-hog barbecue. In Tennessee, a vinegar marinade paired with a tomato-based sauce is the perfect complement to a pork sandwich.

Choosing a method

Whether you decide to use a rub, a brine, a marinade, or a simple seasoning depends on what you're trying to cook and what results you're trying to achieve:

>> **If you want the flavor enhanced throughout the entire muscle of the meat,** soaking it in a brine is a great choice.

>> **If you're trying to cook something with a surface flavor but natural meat flavor throughout the cut,** go with a marinade.

>> **To form a crust on the outer part of your meat that has depth of flavor,** coat the meat with a rub.

TIP

Seasoning is traditionally added after cooking, so you get a brighter flavor because the flavor has not been cooked out of the spices. Adding seasoning afterward is ideal for a West Tennessee dry rib or a barbecue chicken dry-seasoning style.

REMEMBER

You can use a brine and then a seasoning, with pork chops perhaps, or you can marinate a steak and then season it with large-flake salt when you slice and serve it, for example. The combinations are endless — you're limited only by your imagination.

Melding Meat and Liquid: Brines and Marinades

Brines and marinades are liquid ways to season meat. These two different methods can both enhance the flavor of your meat. In the following sections, I explain the difference and when to use each type of wet seasoning.

The juice on brining

Brining is a great way to add flavor to meats. Through the process of *osmosis*, which just means soaking up, you can add moisture as well as flavor throughout the structure of the meat.

Brines come in all flavors and varieties, but let's start with the basics, which is a salt-and-water brine — 1 cup of salt in 1 gallon of water.

TIP

Always use kosher or large-flake salt in a brine so as not to make it too salty.

Beyond the standard saltwater brine, you can venture out and add various flavors to your brine. For example, you can add juices or spices to your brine to kick it up a notch. Just as with rubs, different meats react differently to various brines.

You can use a liquid other than water for your brine, too — apple juice, chicken stock, beef stock, orange juice, wine, and beer are all options. I like to use a saltwater-and-apple-juice brine for pork chops and butts. It adds a flavor that enhances the pork and is still subtle enough not to alter the meat too much.

TIP

Make sure that the container you brine in is plastic or stainless steel and large enough so that you can completely submerge the meat. Stay away from aluminum — it may react badly with the ingredients in your brine.

TIP

Submersion isn't the only brining method. You can also inject liquid into the meat. You just need a brine injector, which looks like a medical syringe but on a much bigger scale. Typically, a brine injector has a needle with a closed end so that the meat doesn't clog the needle as you inject. When injecting a piece of meat, you push the needle deep into the flesh. Push the plunger down as you slowly pull the syringe needle to the outer edge of the meat. Do this in a 1-inch pattern throughout the whole cut of meat.

Making memorable marinades

Marinades are typically used on pieces of meat that don't have a lot of fat on their own. A marinade can help add flavor that comes from fat with other cuts. Marinades come in almost any flavor you can think of — you can use a wide variety of ingredients.

When building a marinade, the three crucial elements are

>> **Fat:** Oil is a great start as a fat. You can use vegetable oil, olive oil, or the oil of your choice.

>> **Acid:** After you've chosen your fat, add your acid. Vinegar, citrus juice, and wine are examples of acids.

>> **Flavor:** Finally, add flavor. Flavor can come in the form of herbs, garlic, soy sauce, Worcestershire sauce, or whatever you like. Choose a flavor you think accentuates the flavor of the meat.

These three elements are the winning combination for any marinade.

BASTING VERSUS MARINATING

Typically, marinade is considered suitable for grilling rather than smoking barbecue. When used for barbecue, a marinade is often called a *baste*.

So, what is a baste? Typically, a baste is a vinegar-based liquid mopped onto meat while it cooks. A typical homemade baste is 5 cups of vinegar, 5 cups of apple juice, and 5 cups of water with 1 tablespoon of oil and a ½ cup of dry seasoning. This is a good, standard baste/marinade for pork or chicken barbecue.

A baste is a way to keep your meat moist. You can use a juice of some sort or a vinegar-based formula. If you use a juice, be sure you're cooking over indirect heat so that the sugars in the juice don't burn the meat.

Some recipes call for you to turn the meat as you baste it. This instruction is usually reserved for smaller pieces of meat you cook quickly or if you're cooking over direct heat. When you cook larger cuts over indirect heat, you seldom turn the meat — you simply don't need to.

Barbecue chefs sometimes use spritz bottles to spray on a baste while cooking ribs or brisket. This helps the meat retain moisture in an environment that tends to get very dry due to the high airflow.

A popular marinade or baste is Wicker's, a vinegar-based marinade that doesn't burn. This quality makes it a popular choice for basting ribs, shoulders, or whole hogs.

Building a Bodacious Rub

When building a rub you want spices that play well together. Use ingredients that you personally like or that enhance the flavor of your meat. In other words, combine spices that complement each other and also complement the meat.

Typical spices in a barbecue rub include salt, pepper, paprika, chili powder, garlic powder, onion powder, and dry mustard. If you want your rub to be sweet, you can add brown or white sugar. With these elements you can make a great basic rub.

There are as many rubs out in the world as there are flavor profiles. You need to find the one that suits your taste, work with it, and perfect it over time. Always write down the ingredients you use in a rub so that you know how to adjust it after you test it out. Never stop experimenting. Your rub may change and may become more complex as you fine-tune the flavors to suit your taste.

Combining salt, sugar, and seasoning

As you're building a rub, start with the basic elements: salt, possibly sugar, and probably other seasonings.

First, you need to decide whether you want a savory rub or a sweet rub. From that point, you build your rub from the ground up.

REMEMBER

The basis of every rub, whether savory or sweet, is salt. You lean more heavily on salt in a savory rub than you do in a sweet one, but salt is the only ingredient that must be in both.

For a sweet rub, sugar (either white or brown) is the most dominant ingredient. You also need salt, but not as much as for a savory rub. You want spices that not only complement the meat but also complement the sweetness of the rub.

For a savory rub, start with salt as the base, and then add pepper. From there you add in elements of flavor that complement the type of meat you're cooking. I offer some basic flavor combos in this book, but other references such as the *Flavor Bible* by Andrew Dornenburg (Little, Brown, & Company) can help you understand what spices work well with what proteins and with what other spices.

TIP

When you taste a rub before cooking with it, you want it to be very bold. You need this. The cooking process along with the fat of the meat tones down the flavors in your rub, so start strong.

Matching rub to meat

Not all rubs go great with all meats; you need to match your rub to your meat.

Beef, for example, has a lot of fat, which is great for flavor but needs to be balanced with something that can cut through the fat. Salt and pepper do just that. They provide balance to the richness of the fat by cutting through it. They create a dynamic balance that results in a flavor like no other.

Pork, although it's fatty, doesn't have the richness of beef, so a different type of rub is in order. With pork, you want to add something that makes a richly flavored bark on the outside. Salt, paprika, brown sugar, mustard powder, and black pepper can all add some more complexity and flavor to your bark.

With pork, the meat is usually pulled or chopped after cooking, so you want a rich exterior crust to blend with the fatty pork and create a flavor sensation.

Poultry is another bird altogether. Chicken is a blank canvas that you can paint any flavor you like on. The even flavor of chicken allows you to add a wide variety of rubs to it, from sweet to savory.

TIP

For a basic seasoning on chicken, try just garlic salt. It adds flavor and also aids in drying and crisping the skin.

Chapter **7**

Finishing Strong: The Sauce

B arbecue sauce is sometimes a controversial subject. In some regions, barbecue sauce is widely accepted as a normal practice. In other regions, not so much. It just depends on where you are.

In the Carolinas, they often say, "We don't use sauce" or "It's not sauced," but they use a vinegar-based sauce typically with hot sauce or red pepper flakes added. Some may consider it a marinade, but others consider it a sauce.

In Memphis, when you get a barbecue sandwich, you can expect it to have sauce and slaw on it. That's the way it's typically served. In Texas, however, sauce can be considered an affront to good barbecue. Most Texas pitmasters like to serve their meats without any sauce so that the meat stands on its own. In Kansas City or Saint Louis, almost everything is sauced, typically with a sauce on the sweeter side.

So, although it doesn't seem like such a controversial subject, barbecue sauce can be just that. From sloppy-joe style to completely naked, there are many, many ways to serve barbecue. To sauce or not to sauce will always be a controversial subject in barbecue.

Building Your Own Sauce

Let's talk about this key element of barbecue. A sauce is a liquid used to enhance the finished product. You get to decide what type of sauce or baste you want to make. The easiest sauce to start with is the typical vinegar-based sauce used throughout all regions of the United States.

WARNING

Most sauces contain sugar, so you need to add the sauce at the very end of the cook or after you take the meat off the grate so that the sugar doesn't burn on the meat. To minimize the chance of burning the sugar into the meat, keep the sugar content in your sauce low.

A baste or mop is typically much thinner than most sauces. Bastes or mop sauces are meant to keep your meat moist while cooking and add an element of flavor. Some bastes or mops, such as a vinegar-based mop, can also be used as a sauce.

Make your sauce or mop to your taste. Some people prefer a tang, and others like it very sweet. A mop or baste is typically tangier in nature, as opposed to a sweet sauce, which is hard to use as a baste because of the sugar content and burn factor.

Choosing a base

You can choose from vinegar, tomato, mustard, or Worcestershire sauce as your base. The next sections explain each option.

Starting with the universal base: Vinegar

The great thing about a vinegar base is that you can use it to easily make a very basic sauce. A vinegar-based sauce tends not to burn on the meat, unlike sauces with sugar, and it has very few ingredients. In order to minimize the ability for a mop or baste to burn, keep out the sugar or keep the sugar content very low.

Start with apple cider vinegar. Add something like apple juice if you like. Don't add too much — you don't want the sugar in the apple juice to burn on the meat in your smoker.

A combination I like as a basic mop sauce and baste is the following:

>> ⅓ cup apple cider vinegar

>> ⅓ cup apple juice

>> ⅓ cup water

To this mixture, you can add a couple of teaspoons of your favorite barbecue seasoning or rub. This gives you a basic base or mop that you can also use as a light vinegar sauce.

When you want to add some heat, add a little cayenne, habanero powder, or red pepper flakes.

When choosing the rub or seasoning to add to this mixture, be sure it doesn't contain a large amount of sugar. Sugar can burn on your meat on the smoker.

Seeing red: A tomato base

For a basic tomato sauce, start with a tomato ketchup and add ingredients from there, starting with a favorite seasoning blend.

This good, simple base can act as a vessel for a spice mixture of your choosing:

>> 2 cups tomato ketchup

>> ¼ cup apple cider vinegar

>> ¼ cup brown sugar

>> ⅛ cup yellow mustard

>> ¼ cup honey

When you get comfortable, start adding your own seasonings as you see fit. I like to line up a table full of spices, get a notebook, and start experimenting. Make sure to document exactly what you added to each of your mixes, and then choose which one you like the best.

Mixing it up with mustard

Mustard sauce is a South Carolina thing and can be quite delicious. Start with a basic recipe like the one here:

>> ¾ cup yellow mustard

>> ½ cup honey

>> ½ cup apple cider vinegar

Then add different ingredients as you see fit. You never know what you might come up with. Let your German roots shine through.

Going tangy with Worcestershire sauce

Barbecue sauce made with Worcestershire sauce isn't all that common, but you do find it in some circles. Typically used for beef barbecue, it has more of a taste for red meat than any other kind of Q.

>> 2 cups ketchup

>> ⅓ cup Worcestershire sauce

>> ½ cup apple cider vinegar

Balancing acid, salt, sweet, and heat

What you should look for in a barbecue sauce is great balance. You want to make sure that the sauce you use complements the meat and the seasoning you're using on the meat.

The basic foundations for sauce are acid, salt, sweet, and heat. (Technically, fat is also an element of this mix, but you have fat in the meat itself, so your sauce needs acidity or sweetness to offset the fattiness of the meat.) Here are the sources for each element:

>> **Acid:** The two main sources for acid are tomatoes (usually in the form of ketchup) and vinegar (often apple cider vinegar). Either ingredient can add the acidity you need for balance in a sauce. You can even use them together, and many pitmasters frequently do.

>> **Salt:** Salting meat brings out its natural flavor. Some people like salt in their rubs, but I personally like to salt the meat first and then go light on the salt in the rub or seasoning. This helps layer the flavors.

>> **Sweet:** The sweet element in barbecue sauce can come from a number of sources — brown sugar is very common, as are honey and molasses. Any of these three ingredients can add the sweetening element many people crave. Some folks like to use turbinado sugar because it's less likely to burn when caramelized on the grill.

>> **Heat:** A great way to spice things up is to add a little heat, as in spiciness, to your barbecue sauce. A great heat source for your sauce is red pepper flakes (typically used in a vinegar-based sauce) or cayenne pepper. Both add heat without being overpowering. If you want to kick up the heat even higher, add some habanero powder.

REMEMBER

Some meats are on the lean side and some are more on the fatty side, so you need to tailor your sauce to the type of meat you're cooking. For example, the more fat that you have on your meat, the more acid you may want in your sauce to balance it out. The acid cuts through the fat and gives you a more balanced flavor.

Using seasonings and spices

When you get more familiar with using spices, you can start to add your own flair. Start with a base from the earlier "Choosing a base" section, or make your own variation and then start adding your spices. Take good notes as you try various combinations.

Use the ten spices in Chapter 19 as a guide for elements to use in your sauce.

TIP

Consider your dry seasoning when developing a sauce. The dry seasoning and your sauce base need to complement each other and create a blended profile that works for the piece of meat you're smoking.

Experimenting as You Go

Don't be afraid to experiment with your sauces, bastes, and rubs. Many of the best rubs you've tasted came from many, many nights of someone experimenting and trying new things.

Broaden your range of ingredients. Go for the unexpected. Variety is the spice of life, and you never know when you might come upon a great new combination.

Leaning on the experts

You can find plenty of resources for sauce-making tips from online sites to numerous cooking shows — even books and magazines.

TIP

Pay attention to the experts. They've already made the mistakes that you're yet to learn from, and they can help you navigate the waters of creating your own unique sauce. Pick up a book from a well-known pitmaster and try the techniques he has used successfully. This book is a great place to start!

Using sauces like a pro

After you develop a sauce of your own, use it correctly. You apply most sauces *after* the meat is cooked.

REMEMBER

If you want to apply barbecue sauce while cooking, make sure that you do it at the end of the process so that it doesn't burn.

WARNING

Don't apply sauce to meat directly over a flame. Most sauces have some sugar, and sugar burns. The last thing you want to do is cook for six hours only to add a sauce and burn it on your meat in the last hour of your cook. You can wrap the meat in foil before applying the sauce if the meat is over direct flame.

If you're using a vinegar-based sauce, you can use it throughout the cook and, depending on what else is in it, it shouldn't burn. That's the benefit of a vinegar-based sauce: It can impart flavor throughout the cooking process without the risk of burning.

3

Barbecue Recipes, Meat by Meat

Steer your way through recipes for beef. Yes, you can cook hamburger barbecue style. You can also smoke beef ribs, meatloaf, and, of course, beef brisket.

Chase chicken and seafood barbecue recipes. Grilled salmon is a taste sensation; so is fresh-smoked trout or red snapper. Splay out a whole spatchcock chicken on the grate, or smoke some wings. Use smoked chicken to make salads, tacos, and pasta dishes.

Spring through barbecue lamb dishes. Smoking lamb chops takes less time than larger pork chops with a distinctive flavor. Most parts of the animal fit on the grill — you can smoke leg of lamb, lamb chops, lamb ribs, a lamb shank, or a rack of lamb.

Pull the barbecue original — pork. In West Tennessee, *barbecue* means pork and pork alone. But other regions of the country choose pork, too. You start with pork butt, which you cook until it pulls off the bone. You can make great barbecue cooking pork ribs, pork loin, ham, or bacon.

Chapter **8**

Beef

Welcome to beef! In this chapter, I talk about cooking everything from whole large cuts down to burgers and bologna. Beef barbecue used to be a purely Texas thing, but that has changed over the years, and you can now find it in almost every region of the United States.

TIP

Beef is readily available at most grocery stores, but you may be able to find the larger cuts only at big-box wholesalers. For specialty cuts like skirt steak or hanger steak, look for a good butcher — these cuts aren't readily available in grocery stores.

BUYING BUTCHER PAPER

Butcher paper — specifically, pink butcher paper — is an essential accessory when cooking some beef cuts. Pink (some may call it red) butcher paper is made with FDA-approved virgin Southern-pine pulp, treated so that it's strong when wet. It's more porous than other butcher paper, so it lets the meat breathe.

Keeping the *bark* (the outer coating of seasonings) crisp is a goal when you cook beef barbecue, and pink butcher paper is ideal for this.

Some recipes tell you to wrap the meat in butcher paper when it reaches an internal temperature that's below the temperature that indicates that the meat is cooked. You wrap the meat and place it back on the grill over indirect heat. You can check the temperature either through the butcher paper or by unwrapping the meat to insert a thermometer.

Whatever you do, don't wrap meat in aluminum foil while it rests. The reflective properties trap the heat so the meat steams as it rests, which makes for a soggy bark.

Beef Brisket

PREP TIME: 30 MIN PLUS 1 HR FOR RESTING	COOK TIME: 16 HR	YIELD: 12 SERVINGS

INGREDIENTS

1 whole beef brisket (USDA Choice or Prime grade)

½ cup kosher large-flake salt

1 cup freshly ground black pepper

16 ounces apple juice

DIRECTIONS

1 Preheat the grill or smoker to 220 degrees.

2 Unwrap the brisket and rinse with cold water.

3 Use a boning knife to trim the brisket, leaving ¼ inch of fat uniformly around the whole brisket.

4 In a bowl, mix the salt and pepper to a uniform consistency.

5 Rub the salt and pepper mixture over the entire brisket, making sure that it's evenly distributed.

6 Place the brisket on the smoker, uncovered, over indirect heat.

7 Pour the apple juice into a spray bottle. Once an hour, spritz the meat with the apple juice, making sure the brisket is thoroughly moistened.

8 Check the temperature of the meat after about 6 hours. When the internal temperature reaches 170 degrees, loosely wrap the brisket in pink butcher paper and place it back on the smoker over indirect heat.

9 Remove the brisket from the smoker when the internal temperature reaches 192 degrees, after about 12 to 16 hours total.

10 Rest the wrapped meat on the counter or in an empty cooler for at least 1 hour before slicing and serving.

PER SERVING: *Calories 419 (From Fat 195); Fat 22g (Saturated 8g); Cholesterol 141mg; Sodium 1,042mg; Carbohydrate 10g (Dietary Fiber 2g); Protein 44g.*

Beef Short Ribs

PREP TIME: ABOUT 10 MIN PLUS 30 MIN FOR RESTING	COOK TIME: 6 HR	YIELD: 4 SERVINGS

INGREDIENTS

1 rack of beef short ribs, about 3 or 4 bones (USDA Choice or Prime grade)

½ cup kosher large-flake salt

1 cup freshly ground black pepper

16 ounces apple juice

DIRECTIONS

1 Preheat the grill or smoker to 250 degrees.

2 Unwrap the short ribs and rinse with cold water.

3 In a bowl, mix the salt and pepper to a uniform consistency.

4 Rub the salt and pepper mixture evenly over the short ribs.

5 Place the ribs on the smoker uncovered over indirect heat.

6 Pour the apple juice into a spray bottle. Once an hour, spritz the meat with the apple juice, making sure the ribs are thoroughly moistened.

7 Check the internal temperature of the ribs after about 2 hours. The ribs will take about 6 hours to reach an internal temperature of 192 degrees.

8 When the internal temperature reaches 192 degrees, take them off the grill and wrap them loosely in butcher paper.

9 Let them rest for 30 minutes; then place them in an empty, insulated cooler for holding.

10 When you're ready to serve, remove the ribs from the cooler, unwrap them, slice them, and enjoy.

PER SERVING: *Calories 368 (From Fat 250); Fat 28g (Saturated 12g); Cholesterol 62mg; Sodium 3,264mg; Carbohydrate 14g (Dietary Fiber 0g); Protein 14g.*

Smoked Prime Rib

PREP TIME: 30 MIN PLUS 30 MIN FOR RESTING	COOK TIME: 4 HR	YIELD: 10 SERVINGS

INGREDIENTS

1 whole rib roast, 8 to 13 pounds (USDA Choice or Prime grade)

¼ cup kosher salt

¼ cup cracked black pepper

¼ cup fresh rosemary

¼ cup fresh thyme

½ cup olive oil

DIRECTIONS

1 Preheat the grill or smoker to 250 degrees.

2 Unwrap the rib roast and rinse with cold water.

3 Trim the rib roast to leave ¼ inch of fat uniformly around the top of the roast. Try to trim any silver skin or sinew from the rib side of the roast.

4 In a bowl, mix the salt, pepper, rosemary, and thyme to a uniform consistency.

5 Rub down the rib roast evenly with the olive oil.

6 Rub the spice mixture evenly over the entire roast.

7 Place the rib roast on the smoker, uncovered, over indirect heat.

8 Check the meat temperature every hour. You're shooting for an internal temperature of 140 degrees.

9 When the meat reaches 140 degrees (after about 3 to 4 hours), remove it from the smoker and allow it to rest for 30 minutes.

10 Slice, serve, and enjoy.

PER SERVING: *Calories 676 (From Fat 436); Fat 48g (Saturated 16g); Cholesterol 165mg; Sodium 1,651mg; Carbohydrate 0g (Dietary Fiber 0g); Protein 56g.*

TIP: When you cook ribs of any description, first remove the membrane on the inside (the ridged side) of the ribs. Called *silver skin,* this membrane doesn't add flavor to the meat, and it can act as a barrier to your rub and smoke.

Smoked Tri Tip

PREP TIME: 30 MIN PLUS 30 MIN FOR RESTING	COOK TIME: 45–90 MIN	YIELD: 4 SERVINGS

INGREDIENTS

1 tri tip roast, 2 to 2½ pounds (USDA Choice or Prime grade)

¼ cup kosher salt

¼ cup fresh cracked black pepper

¼ cup fresh rosemary

¼ cup fresh thyme

DIRECTIONS

1 Preheat the grill or smoker to 250 degrees.

2 Unwrap the rib roast and rinse with cold water.

3 Trim the roast to leave ¼ inch of fat uniformly around the top of the roast and try to trim any silver skin or sinew from the rib side of the roast.

4 In a bowl, mix the salt, pepper, rosemary, and thyme to a uniform consistency.

5 Rub the spice mixture evenly over the entire roast.

6 Place on the smoker, uncovered, over indirect heat.

7 Check the meat temperature every hour. You're shooting for an internal temperature of 140 degrees.

8 When the meat reaches 140 degrees, remove it from the smoker and allow it to rest for 30 minutes.

9 Slice, serve, and enjoy.

PER SERVING: *Calories 490 (From Fat 247); Fat 27g (Saturated 10g); Cholesterol 208mg; Sodium 3,471mg; Carbohydrate 0g (Dietary Fiber 0g); Protein 57g.*

TIP: When you cook ribs of any description, first remove the membrane on the inside (the ridged side) of the ribs. Called *silver skin,* this membrane doesn't add flavor to the meat, and it can act as a barrier to your rub and smoke.

Smoked Burger

INGREDIENTS

2 pounds ground beef or ground chuck (80 percent or 90 percent lean)

1 teaspoon kosher salt

1 teaspoon fine cracked black pepper

Additional spice of your choosing (garlic powder or onion powder, for example)

DIRECTIONS

1 Preheat the grill or smoker to 220 degrees.

2 In a bowl, place the ground beef, salt, and pepper.

3 Add any other seasonings you like, and thoroughly mix.

4 Form uniform patties, about 8 ounces each. The burgers should be about 1 inch thick and completely uniform. *Note:* The more you handle them, the more they bind together from the heat of your hands, which is what you want.

5 Place the burgers over indirect heat.

6 Check the burgers' temperature every 15 minutes. You're looking for an internal temperature of around 140 degrees (about 30 to 60 minutes total).

7 Remove the burgers and serve on a bun with your favorite condiments.

PER SERVING: *Calories 372 (From Fat 200); Fat 22g (Saturated 9g); Cholesterol 139mg; Sodium 395mg; Carbohydrate 0g (Dietary Fiber 0g); Protein 40g.*

Smoked Bologna

PREP TIME: ABOUT 10 MIN	COOK TIME: 2 HR	YIELD: 6 SERVINGS

INGREDIENTS

1 large chub of all-beef bologna

1 cup yellow mustard

Basic BBQ Rub (see Chapter 12)

DIRECTIONS

1 Preheat the grill or smoker to 220 degrees.

2 Cut a crosshatch pattern in the bologna all around the whole chub, about ¼-inch deep.

3 Slather the entire chub with the yellow mustard.

4 Rub down the chub with Basic BBQ Rub.

5 Place on the smoker on indirect heat.

6 Smoke for 2 hours. Remember that the bologna is already cooked, so don't smoke it too long or too hot.

7 Remove the bologna from the smoker and let cool.

8 Cut the bologna into rounds and serve as is or cut into rounds and then grill it before serving.

PER SERVING: *Calories 575 (From Fat 417); Fat 46g (Saturated 17g); Cholesterol 85mg; Sodium 2,720mg; Carbohydrate 25g (Dietary Fiber 6g); Protein 19g.*

NOTE: A *chub* is a tube of meat, like a sausage roll.

Smoked Beef Tenderloin with Blue Cheese Butter

PREP TIME: ABOUT 20 MIN, PLUS 15 MIN FOR RESTING	COOK TIME: 45 MIN	YIELD: 6 SERVINGS

INGREDIENTS

1 whole beef tenderloin

¼ cup olive oil, to coat the meat

¼ cup Steak Seasoning (see Chapter 12)

4 ounces crumbled blue cheese, at room temperature

¼ cup salted butter, at room temperature

DIRECTIONS

1 Preheat the grill or smoker to 275 degrees.

2 Trim the tenderloin, removing the excess fat and the silver skin. Rub the tenderloin with the olive oil and then with the Steak Seasoning.

3 Place the tenderloin on the smoker over indirect heat.

4 Smoke until the meat reaches an internal temp of 120 degrees.

5 Move the tenderloin over to direct heat and sear the outside.

6 Cook until the internal temperature reaches 135 degrees.

7 In a small bowl, add the softened butter and blue cheese. Mix thoroughly with a fork.

8 When the tenderloin is finished cooking, take it off the heat and let it rest for 15 minutes.

9 Slice the tenderloin and serve with the blue cheese and butter mixture.

PER SERVING: *Calories 614 (From Fat 386); Fat 44g (Saturated 17g); Cholesterol 173mg; Sodium 2,873mg; Carbohydrate 3g (Dietary Fiber 2g); Protein 50g.*

TIP: When you trim your tenderloin, make sure to remove the silvery membrane. Called *silver skin,* this membrane doesn't add flavor to the meat, and it can act as a barrier to your rub and smoke.

Steak Fajitas

PREP TIME: 6 HR   COOK TIME: 20 MIN   YIELD: 8 SERVINGS

INGREDIENTS

½ cup olive oil

½ cup soy sauce

¼ cup fresh minced garlic

½ cup lime juice

1 tablespoon cumin

1 tablespoon chili powder

1 tablespoon black pepper

½ cup light brown sugar

2 pounds skirt steak, trimmed and thinly sliced across the grain

1 whole bell pepper cut into ¼-inch strips

1 whole yellow onion peeled and sliced into ¼-inch slices

Eight 6-inch flour tortillas

DIRECTIONS

1 In a bowl, add olive oil, soy sauce, garlic, lime juice, cumin, chili powder, black pepper, and brown sugar, and mix thoroughly. Set aside ½ cup of this mixture.

2 Put the rest of the mixture into a resealable bag and add the steak.

3 Marinate for 3 to 6 hours.

4 Preheat the grill or smoker to 350 degrees.

5 Place the steak over direct heat and turn often to prevent burning.

6 When the meat reaches an internal temperature of 140 degrees, remove it from the heat and let it rest.

7 While the steak is resting, add the bell peppers and onions to a cast-iron skillet over direct heat, and sauté until soft.

8 Add the steak along with the remainder of the marinade to the bell peppers and onions and mix.

9 Lay out the tortillas, place one-eighth of the fajita mixture on each tortilla roll, and serve warm.

PER SERVING: *Calories 491 (From Fat 235); Fat 26g (Saturated 6g); Cholesterol 56mg; Sodium 1,285mg; Carbohydrate 37g (Dietary Fiber 2g); Protein 27g.*

Chapter 9

Chicken and Seafood

n this chapter, I talk all things chicken. Chicken is a staple of barbecue in every region, and it's a welcome addition to any summer barbecue.

REMEMBER

Temperature is always key with chicken: The safety of the meal depends on the chicken reaching an internal temperature of 165 degrees. When checking the temperature, I aim for the thickest part of the bird — the thigh, not the breast, if you're cooking a whole bird or half a bird. You don't want the juices to run out of the breast.

I also touch on seafood in this chapter. Although not often thought of as barbecue, seafood can be a healthy addition to your menu.

TIP

I often cook seafood on a cedar plank to impart some flavor or use a grill basket so that the delicate meat doesn't fall through the cracks of the grate. (See Chapter 3 for descriptions of grilling accessories.)

BBQ Chicken

INGREDIENTS

2 whole chickens

¼ cup garlic salt

½ cup Basic BBQ Sauce
(see Chapter 13)

DIRECTIONS

1 Preheat the grill or smoker to 275 degrees.

2 Cut the chickens in half lengthwise, from the neck to the tail.

3 Sprinkle the chicken halves with garlic salt on both sides.

4 Place the chicken halves on indirect heat in your smoker or grill.

5 Check the chicken every 30 minutes to make sure your fire is at the proper temperature.

6 After 1½ hours, check the temperature of the chicken by inserting a meat thermometer in the back of the thigh. You want an internal temperature of 165 degrees.

7 When the chicken reaches 165 degrees, slather it with the sauce. (You do this last because the sauce will burn if you're not careful.)

8 Give the sauce enough time to warm up on the bird, about 5 minutes, and then pull it from the grill and serve hot.

PER SERVING: *Calories 609 (From Fat 300); Fat 32g (Saturated 8g); Cholesterol 243mg; Sodium 2,839mg; Carbohydrate 23g (Dietary Fiber 0g); Protein 63g.*

TIP: If you don't have time to make the Basic BBQ Sauce, you can use your favorite commercial barbecue sauce instead.

Whole Smoked Chicken

PREP TIME: 30 MIN	COOK TIME: 2 HR	YIELD: 8 SERVINGS

INGREDIENTS

2 whole chickens

Coarse-ground salt to taste

Coarse-ground pepper to taste

2 cups Basic BBQ Sauce (see Chapter 13)

2 large oranges, quartered

2 large onions, quartered

2 tablespoons garlic salt

DIRECTIONS

1 Preheat the grill or smoker to 275 degrees.

2 Clean the chickens by rinsing them under cold water and removing the giblets and necks.

3 Fill your hand with a 50/50 mixture of salt and pepper and thoroughly rub the inside of the birds.

4 Place 1 quartered orange and 1 quartered onion in the cavity of each bird. Stuff the birds full.

5 Sprinkle the skin of the birds with garlic salt.

6 Place the chickens on indirect heat in your smoker or grill.

7 Check the chicken every 30 minutes to make sure that your grill temperature is still at 275 degrees.

8 After 2 hours, check the temperature of the chicken by inserting a meat thermometer in the back of the thigh. You want an internal temperature of 165 degrees.

9 When the chicken reaches 165 degrees, remove it from the grill or smoker, let it rest for 20 minutes, and serve hot.

PER SERVING: *Calories 534 (From Fat 206); Fat 23g (Saturated 6g); Cholesterol 182mg; Sodium 2,311mg; Carbohydrate 33g (Dietary Fiber 2g); Protein 47g.*

TIP: If you don't have time to make the Basic BBQ Sauce, you can use your favorite commercial barbecue sauce instead.

Spatchcock Chicken

PREP TIME: 30 MIN	COOK TIME: 1 HR	YIELD: 4 SERVINGS

INGREDIENTS

1 whole chicken

½ cup Chicken Rub
(see Chapter 12)

DIRECTIONS

1 Preheat the grill or smoker to 275 degrees.

2 Clean the chicken by rinsing it under cold water and removing the giblets and neck.

3 Roll the bird onto the breast side and cut the back of the chicken from head to tail. *Do not cut through the breast side.*

4 Pull the chicken open so that it lays flat with both legs kicked out.

5 Sprinkle the rub on the bird and thoroughly rub it into both sides.

6 Place the chicken on direct heat on the grill. Add the chips or chucks of hickory to your fire. Watch the chicken closely because it's over direct heat. You may want to turn the bird every 15 minutes to make sure it cooks evenly.

7 After 45 minutes, check the temperature of the chicken by inserting a meat thermometer in the back of the thigh. You want an internal temperature of 165 degrees.

8 When the chicken reaches 165 degrees, remove it from the grill or smoker, let it rest for 20 minutes, and serve hot.

PER SERVING: *Calories 402 (From Fat 204); Fat 23g (Saturated 6g); Cholesterol 182mg; Sodium 11,895mg; Carbohydrate 0g (Dietary Fiber 0g); Protein 46g.*

NOTE: A *spatchcock chicken* is simply a whole chicken cut along the spine to lay out flat.

Smoked Wings

PREP TIME: ABOUT 10 MIN | COOK TIME: 45 MIN | YIELD: 6 SERVINGS

INGREDIENTS

12 whole chicken wings or pieces

1 tablespoon garlic salt

2 quarts cooking oil for deep frying

1 cup Basic BBQ Sauce (see Chapter 13)

4 ounces ranch or blue cheese dressing, for dipping

DIRECTIONS

1 Preheat the grill or smoker to 275 degrees.

2 Lay out the chicken wings and sprinkle them with garlic salt.

3 Place the wings on indirect heat in your smoker or grill. Add chips or chunks of hickory to your fire.

4 Check on the wings every 15 minutes and add chips to the fire if needed.

5 After 45 minutes, check the temperature of the wings by inserting a meat thermometer into the thickest part of the meat. You want an internal temperature of 165 degrees.

6 When the chicken reaches 165 degrees, remove it from the grill or smoker and let it cool at room temperature for 10 minutes.

7 Fill a skillet, fryer, or deep pot with enough oil to submerge the wings. If you have a deep fryer, use it.

8 Heat the oil to 350 degrees.

9 Carefully submerge the wings into the oil using a basket or fryer strainer, and fry for 5 minutes.

10 Remove from the fryer and let drain.

11 Toss the wings in the Basic BBQ Sauce.

12 Serve with a side of either blue cheese or ranch dressing.

PER SERVING: *Calories 357 (From Fat 219); Fat 24g (Saturated 5g); Cholesterol 76mg; Sodium 2,256mg; Carbohydrate 16g (Dietary Fiber 0g); Protein 17g.*

TIP: If you don't have time to make the Basic BBQ Sauce, you can use your favorite commercial barbecue sauce instead.

Smoked Chicken Salad

PREP TIME: 30 MIN	COOK TIME: NONE	YIELD: 6 SERVINGS

INGREDIENTS

1 quart BBQ Chicken (see recipe earlier in this chapter)

1 cup diced yellow onion, ¼-inch dice

1 cup diced green apple, ¼-inch dice

1 cup diced celery, ¼-inch dice

1 cup mayonnaise

Coarse-ground salt to taste

Coarse-ground black pepper to taste

DIRECTIONS

1 In a large mixing bowl, add the chicken, onion, apple, celery, and mayonnaise; mix thoroughly.

2 Add the salt and pepper.

3 Chill for at least 2 hours, and serve cold.

PER SERVING: *Calories 912 (From Fat 563); Fat 61g (Saturated 11g); Cholesterol 265mg; Sodium 2,003mg; Carbohydrate 28g (Dietary Fiber 7g); Protein 64g.*

Smoked Chicken Tacos

PREP TIME: ABOUT 10 MIN	COOK TIME: 45 MIN	YIELD: 8 SERVINGS

INGREDIENTS

4 boneless chicken thighs

¼ cup Chicken Rub (see Chapter 12)

Eight 6-inch flour tortillas

1 cup diced onions

2 cups shredded cabbage

½ cup minced cilantro

1 cup Alabama White Sauce (see Chapter 13)

DIRECTIONS

1 Preheat the grill or smoker to 275 degrees.

2 Rub the thighs with the Chicken Rub.

3 Place the thighs on indirect heat in your smoker or grill. Add chips or chunks of hickory to your fire.

4 Check on the thighs every 15 minutes and add chips to the fire if needed.

5 After 30 minutes, check the temperature of the thighs by inserting a meat thermometer into the thickest part of the meat. You want an internal temperature of 165 degrees.

6 When the chicken reaches 165 degrees, remove it from the grill or smoker and let it rest.

7 Dice the chicken into ½-inch pieces and set aside.

8 To assemble the tacos, lay out the tortillas; then place ⅛ of the chicken (a small handful) on each tortilla. Add ⅛ of the diced onion and the shredded cabbage. Top off with a sprinkle of cilantro and a drizzle of Alabama White Sauce. Fold in half and serve.

PER SERVING: *Calories 356 (From Fat 223); Fat 24g (Saturated 4g); Cholesterol 42mg; Sodium 3,288mg; Carbohydrate 23g (Dietary Fiber 2g); Protein 11g.*

Dutch-Oven Smoked, Baked Chicken

PREP TIME: ABOUT 10 MIN	COOK TIME: 1–1½ HR	YIELD: 6 SERVINGS

INGREDIENTS

4 cups chicken stock

2 cups uncooked rice

1 cup diced onions
(¼-inch dice)

1 cup diced celery (¼-inch dice)

1 cup diced carrots (¼-inch dice)

¼ cup minced garlic

6 bone-in chicken thighs

¼ cup Chicken Rub
(see Chapter 12)

Coarse-ground salt to taste

Coarse-ground black pepper to taste

DIRECTIONS

1 Preheat the grill or smoker to 300 degrees with a good bed of coals on one side of the grill.

2 To a Dutch oven, add the chicken stock, rice, onion, celery, carrots, and garlic, and place it directly in the coals.

3 Rub the chicken thighs with the Chicken Rub.

4 Place the thighs on the opposite side of the grill over indirect heat. Add chips or chunks of hickory to your fire.

5 After the thighs have smoked for 15 minutes, open the Dutch oven and place the thighs on top of the rice mixture.

6 Close the lid and use tongs to move some coals on top of the lid of the Dutch oven.

7 Let the mixture cook for 45 – 60 more minutes in the fire; then remove the Dutch oven and set aside for 20 minutes.

8 Remove the lid and check the temperature of the chicken by inserting a meat thermometer into the thickest part of the thighs. You want the thighs to have an internal temperature of at least 165 degrees and the rice to be cooked.

9 Serve hot.

PER SERVING: Calories 465 (From Fat 108); Fat 12g (Saturated 3g); Cholesterol 62mg; Sodium 4,237mg; Carbohydrate 62g (Dietary Fiber 2g); Protein 25g.

Smoked Chicken Pasta

PREP TIME: 30 MIN	COOK TIME: NONE	YIELD: 6 SERVINGS

INGREDIENTS

12 ounces spaghetti or angel-hair pasta

½ cup diced bacon with 2 tablespoons of grease reserved

1 tablespoon olive oil

1 tablespoon minced garlic

3 cups baby spinach

2 cups diced tomatoes

½ cup heavy cream

⅓ cup freshly grated Parmesan cheese

Coarse-ground salt to taste

Coarse-ground black pepper to taste

1 pint Whole Smoked Chicken, pulled or diced (see recipe earlier in this chapter)

DIRECTIONS

1 Cook the pasta to the texture of your liking. Drain and set aside.

2 In a cast-iron skillet, cook the bacon. Because it's diced, it will cook quickly — constantly stir the bacon so it doesn't burn. Drain the grease saving approximately 2 tablespoons. Set the bacon aside to cool.

3 In a large sauté pan, add the olive oil and garlic, and lightly sauté the garlic until it starts to slightly brown.

4 Add the spinach and tomatoes and sauté until the spinach wilts.

5 Add the cream and Parmesan and cook over medium heat, stirring constantly, until a smooth consistency is reached.

6 Add the salt and pepper.

7 Add the pasta, bacon, bacon grease, and chicken. Stir everything together and heat for 3 to 5 minutes.

8 Serve hot.

PER SERVING: *Calories 762 (From Fat 304); Fat 34g (Saturated 12g); Cholesterol 163mg; Sodium 1,785mg; Carbohydrate 69g (Dietary Fiber 4g); Protein 44g.*

Smoked Fried Chicken Sammy

PREP TIME: ABOUT 10 MIN | COOK TIME: 40 MIN | YIELD: 6 SERVINGS

INGREDIENTS

6 boneless, skin-on chicken thighs

½ cup Chicken Rub, divided (see Chapter 12)

2 eggs

2 cups buttermilk

2 cups all-purpose flour

Coarse-ground salt to taste

1 tablespoon coarse-ground black pepper

2 quarts vegetable oil for deep frying

DIRECTIONS

1 Preheat the grill or smoker to 250 degrees.

2 Lay out the thighs on a baking sheet and season them thoroughly with ¼ cup of the rub.

3 Place on the smoker over indirect heat, and cook to an internal temperature of 145 degrees. Remove from the smoker and let cool.

4 In a shallow dish, beat the eggs and then mix in the buttermilk.

5 In another shallow dish, add the flour, the remaining ¼ cup of the rub, and the pepper; mix evenly.

6 Dredge each piece of chicken in the buttermilk wash and then dredge in the flour mixture.

7 Fill your skillet with frying oil and heat the oil to a temperature of 350 degrees.

8 Carefully drop each piece of chicken in the fryer individually for 6 minutes or until the internal temperature reaches 165 degrees.

9 Remove from the fryer and serve on a bun.

PER SERVING: *Calories 416 (From Fat 135); Fat 15g (Saturated 5g); Cholesterol 110mg; Sodium 8,392mg; Carbohydrate 36g (Dietary Fiber 1g); Protein 32g.*

TIP: Add mayonnaise, lettuce, and a pickle for a great sammy.

Smoked Salmon

PREP TIME: ABOUT 10 MIN | COOK TIME: 40 MIN | YIELD: 4 SERVINGS

INGREDIENTS

1 side of salmon

¼ cup maple syrup

¼ cup Basic BBQ Rub
(see Chapter 12)

DIRECTIONS

1 Preheat the smoker to 220 degrees.

2 Place the salmon on a cedar plank, skin side down, and place the plank over indirect heat on your smoker.

3 Every 5 minutes, baste the salmon with the maple syrup.

4 After the third glaze, sprinkle the rub on the salmon.

5 Cook to an internal temperature of 140 degrees.

6 Remove from the smoker and serve hot.

PER SERVING: *Calories 774 (From Fat 277); Fat 31g (Saturated 4g); Cholesterol 249mg; Sodium 817mg; Carbohydrate 14g (Dietary Fiber 0g); Protein 92g.*

New Orleans–Style BBQ Shrimp

PREP TIME: ABOUT 20 MIN	COOK TIME: 40 MIN	YIELD: 6 SERVINGS

INGREDIENTS

½ cup butter

½ cup olive oil

½ cup Worcestershire sauce

¼ cup minced white onion

1 tablespoon Cajun seasoning (unsalted)

4 cloves garlic, minced

⅛ cup fresh minced parsley

1 teaspoon dried or ¼ cup fresh oregano

1 teaspoon dried or ¼ cup fresh thyme

3 pounds fresh, unpeeled shrimp, head on if possible

DIRECTIONS

1 Preheat the grill or smoker to 350 degrees.

2 To a saucepan, add all the ingredients except the shrimp.

3 Heat on low until the butter is melted and the liquids and spices are thoroughly blended.

4 In a cast-iron skillet, place the shrimp. Pour the butter mixture evenly over the shrimp.

5 Place the uncovered skillet on the grill on indirect heat.

6 Stirring every 5 minutes, cook until the shrimp start to turn pink and curl slightly.

7 Serve hot in the skillet with fresh French bread.

PER SERVING: *Calories 524 (From Fat 330); Fat 27g (Saturated 13g); Cholesterol 328mg; Sodium 616mg; Carbohydrate 9g (Dietary Fiber 0g); Protein 39g.*

Poached BBQ Shrimp

INGREDIENTS

2 pounds unpeeled fresh shrimp, head on if possible

16 ounces Basic BBQ Sauce (see Chapter 13)

DIRECTIONS

1 Preheat the grill or smoker to 350 degrees.

2 In a cast-iron skillet, spread the shrimp evenly. Pour the barbecue sauce over the shrimp.

3 Place the uncovered skillet on the grill on indirect heat, stirring every 5 minutes.

4 Cook until the shrimp start to turn pink and curl slightly.

5 Serve hot in the skillet with fresh French bread.

PER SERVING: *Calories 398 (From Fat 34); Fat 4g (Saturated 1g); Cholesterol 302mg; Sodium 1,692mg; Carbohydrate 47g (Dietary Fiber 1g); Protein 40g.*

TIP: If you don't have time to make the Basic BBQ Sauce, you can use your favorite commercial barbecue sauce instead.

Whole Grilled Fish

PREP TIME: ABOUT 20 MIN | COOK TIME: 40 MIN | YIELD: 4 SERVINGS

INGREDIENTS

1 cleaned and descaled fish (red snapper, trout, or yellowfin snapper)

Coarse-ground salt to coat the fish inside and out

Coarse-ground black pepper to coat the fish inside and out

1 lemon sliced into thin rounds

2 sprigs fresh or 1 teaspoon dried dill

¼ cup olive oil

½ cup Chimichurri (see Chapter 13)

DIRECTIONS

1 Preheat the grill or smoker to 350 degrees.

2 Salt and pepper the inner cavity of the fish.

3 Cut three diagonal, parallel slits on the top outer skin of the fish on both sides.

4 Fill the cavity with 3 to 4 lemon slices and the dill.

5 Coat the outside of the fish thoroughly with olive oil.

6 Salt and pepper to taste.

7 Make sure your grill surface is very clean and well oiled.

8 Place the fish on direct heat.

9 Cook the fish for about 10 minutes. Don't try to turn it too quickly. Let the fish sear enough to release from the grill grate.

10 Slowly flip the fish with a spatula or tongs on the backbone side of the fish. If you flip on the cavity side, your contents and juices may spill out.

11 Continue to cook for about 10 minutes until the internal temperature at the thickest part is 135 degrees.

12 Remove from the grill, place on a plate, drizzle on the chimichurri, and serve hot.

PER SERVING: *Calories 325 (From Fat 238); Fat 26g (Saturated 4g); Cholesterol 50mg; Sodium 483mg; Carbohydrate 3g (Dietary Fiber 0g); Protein 17g.*

NOTE: The fish should come cleaned from your provider with the belly open.

Chapter **10**

Lamb

You don't always associate lamb with barbecue, but it can be a delicious addition to your barbecue menu. Just ask the people of Kentucky about their mutton or *burgoo* (essentially, a thick stew). Lamb cuts are generally smaller than other meats, because it's a smaller animal, so cook times are shorter.

TECHNICAL
STUFF

Lamb is technically defined as a sheep in its first year, so it's young meat. *Mutton* is meat from sheep older than two years.

I hope the recipes in this chapter convince you to add lamb to your repertoire. Its wonderful flavor and international appeal make lamb essential to any barbecue tradition.

Smoked Leg of Lamb

PREP TIME: 30 MIN	COOK TIME: 3–4 HR	YIELD: 12 SERVINGS

INGREDIENTS

1 leg of lamb

½ cup olive oil

¼ cup Dijon mustard

¼ cup fresh or 4 teaspoons dried rosemary

¼ cup fresh or 4 teaspoons dried thyme

¼ cup fresh minced garlic

DIRECTIONS

1 Preheat the grill or smoker to 250 degrees.

2 Let the lamb sit out and reach room temperature.

3 In the bowl of a food processor, add the olive oil, mustard, rosemary, thyme, and garlic and pulse until thoroughly blended.

4 Slather the mixture all over the leg of lamb.

5 Place the lamb on the smoker on indirect heat and smoke for 3 to 4 hours.

6 Check the temperature after 2½ hours. When the internal temperature registers 145 degrees, remove the lamb from the heat and let it rest for 30 minutes.

7 Slice and serve hot.

PER SERVING: *Calories 335 (From Fat 207); Fat 23g (Saturated 8g); Cholesterol 103mg; Sodium 133mg; Carbohydrate 2g (Dietary Fiber 1g); Protein 29g.*

Beef Brisket (Chapter 8)

Smoked Bologna (Chapter 8)

Wet Ribs (Chapter 11) with Basic Mop Sauce (Chapter 13)

Smoked Wings (Chapter 9) with Alabama
White Sauce (Chapter 13)

**BBQ Chicken (Chapter 9)
with Basic BBQ
Rub (Chapter 12)**

**Smoked Salmon (Chapter 9)
with Basic BBQ
Rub (Chapter 12)**

Smoked Chicken Salad (Chapter 9) with Pimento Cheese (Chapter 14)

BBQ Pork Butt (Pulled Pork) (Chapter 11)

Dry Ribs (Chapter 11) with Basic BBQ Rub (Chapter 12)

Basic BBQ Rub (Chapter 12)

Pimento Cheese (Chapter 14)

BBQ Beans (Chapter 15)

Mac and Cheese (Chapter 15)

Blueberry Pie (Chapter 16)

Grilled Peaches with Smoked Whipped Cream (Chapter 16)

Lamb Kabobs

PREP TIME: 1½ HR	COOK TIME: 20 MIN	YIELD: 4 SERVINGS

INGREDIENTS

1 pound cubed, boneless lamb shoulder

½ cup olive oil plus enough to coat the meat

¼ cup Dijon mustard

¼ cup fresh rosemary

¼ cup fresh thyme

¼ cup fresh garlic

2 whole green bell peppers cut into 1-inch cubes

2 whole red bell peppers cut into 1-inch cubes

2 large onions cut into 1-inch cubes

2 cups pineapple, cubed

6 cups cooked rice

DIRECTIONS

1 Preheat the grill or smoker to 300 degrees.

2 Let the lamb sit out and reach room temperature.

3 In the bowl of a food processor, add the ½ cup of olive oil, mustard, rosemary, thyme, and garlic and pulse until thoroughly blended.

4 Place half the mixture in a large resealable bag.

5 Add the lamb to the bag and marinate for an hour in the refrigerator.

6 Place the meat, bell peppers, onions, and pineapple on the skewers, alternating the vegetables and fruit with the meat.

7 Place the skewers on the grill over direct heat and watch carefully.

8 Baste the skewers with the other half of the marinade as they cook.

9 Turn the skewers as needed to cook evenly.

10 When the meat on the skewers hits an internal temperature of 145 degrees, remove them from the heat.

11 Remove the food from the skewers and serve over the rice.

PER SERVING: *Calories 850 (From Fat 346); Fat 38g (Saturated 7g); Cholesterol 72mg; Sodium 536mg; Carbohydrate 97g (Dietary Fiber 8g); Protein 31g.*

Lamb Chops

INGREDIENTS

4 lamb chops

¼ cup Lamb Rub (see Chapter 12)

¼ cup mint

1 cup olive oil

1 tablespoon lemon juice

DIRECTIONS

1 Preheat the grill to 300 degrees.

2 Let the lamb sit out and reach room temperature.

3 In the bowl of a food processor, add the mint, olive oil, and lemon juice and pulse a few times to blend; set aside.

4 Rub each chop with the Lamb Rub.

5 Place the lamb chops over direct heat on the grill.

6 Brush the chops with the mint oil as they're grilling. Flip the chops once, halfway through cooking, about 3 to 5 minutes in.

7 Remove the chops from the flames when they reach an internal temperature of 145 degrees, or at your desired doneness.

8 Drizzle with the remaining mint oil and serve.

PER SERVING: *Calories 857 (From Fat 731); Fat 82g (Saturated 19g); Cholesterol 104mg; Sodium 2,675mg; Carbohydrate 9g (Dietary Fiber 3g); Protein 25g.*

TIP: Lamb chops cook very quickly because they're so small. Keep a close eye on the chops as they're cooking.

Rack of Lamb

PREP TIME: 30 MIN	COOK TIME: 45–60 MIN	YIELD: 4 SERVINGS

INGREDIENTS

1 rack of lamb

½ cup olive oil

½ cup Steak Seasoning (see Chapter 12)

DIRECTIONS

1 Preheat the grill or smoker to 250 degrees.

2 Let the lamb sit out and reach room temperature.

3 Slather the rack of lamb with the olive oil.

4 Rub the Steak Seasoning all over the rack of lamb.

5 Place the lamb on the smoker on indirect heat and smoke for 30 to 45 minutes.

6 When the internal temperature reaches 125 degrees, move the rack to the direct-heat side of the grill and sear on all sides.

7 When the meat reaches an internal temperature of 145 degrees, remove it from the heat and let it rest for 10 minutes.

8 Slice and serve hot.

PER SERVING: *Calories 593 (From Fat 500); Fat 56g (Saturated 16g); Cholesterol 93mg; Sodium 1,682mg; Carbohydrate 0g (Dietary Fiber 0g); Protein 3g.*

Smoked Lamb Meatballs

PREP TIME: 30 MIN	COOK TIME: 1HR 20 MIN	YIELD: 4 SERVINGS

INGREDIENTS

1 pound ground lamb

1 egg

½ cup minced onion

½ cup breadcrumbs

½ cup fresh, minced parsley

1 teaspoon coarse ground salt

1 teaspoon coarse ground pepper

1 tablespoon fresh minced garlic

1 tablespoon Lamb Rub (see Chapter 12)

DIRECTIONS

1 Preheat the grill or smoker to 250 degrees.

2 In a large mixing bowl, add all the ingredients and mix together thoroughly.

3 Place in the refrigerator to chill for 20 minutes.

4 Remove from the refrigerator and roll into balls about 1 inch in diameter. You should end up with 8 meatballs.

5 Place the meatballs on the smoker over indirect heat.

6 Smoke for about 1 hour and 20 minutes, until firm and the internal temperature reaches at least 145 degrees.

7 Remove and serve.

PER SERVING: *Calories 393 (From Fat 246); Fat 27g (Saturated 12g); Cholesterol 83mg; Sodium 908mg; Carbohydrate 13g (Dietary Fiber 1g); Protein 22g.*

Smoked Lamb on Pita

PREP TIME: 20 MIN	COOK TIME: 30 MIN	YIELD: 4 SERVINGS

INGREDIENTS

1 tablespoon olive oil

½ medium cucumber, peeled and diced

1 teaspoon minced garlic

2 cups plain yogurt

1 lemon, juiced

½ teaspoon coarse ground salt

2 pieces pita bread

4 large leaves romaine lettuce

8 Lamb Meatballs (see the recipe in this chapter)

1 large tomato, diced

DIRECTIONS

1   In the bowl of a food processor, add the olive oil, cucumber, garlic, yogurt, lemon juice, and salt and pulse until thoroughly blended; set aside.

2   Cut each piece of pita bread in half.

3   Stuff a lettuce leaf into each pita pocket. Add two lamb meatballs and one-quarter of the diced tomatoes to each pocket.

4   Scoop 1 to 2 tablespoons of the yogurt sauce into each pocket and serve.

PER SERVING: *Calories 598 (From Fat 298); Fat 33g (Saturated 13g); Cholesterol 90mg; Sodium 1,449mg; Carbohydrate 42g (Dietary Fiber 3g); Protein 32g.*

Grilled Braised Lamb Shank

PREP TIME: 30 MIN	COOK TIME: 3 HR	YIELD: 4 SERVINGS

INGREDIENTS

4 lamb shanks

2 teaspoons olive oil, plus enough to coat the shanks

½ cup Steak Seasoning (see Chapter 12)

¼ cup minced garlic

1 large white onion, diced

2 large carrots, peeled and cut into ½-inch rounds

¼ cup flour

2 teaspoons Italian seasoning

1 bay leaf

2 cups tomato sauce

2 teaspoons tomato paste

1½ cups red wine of your choice

2 cups beef stock

DIRECTIONS

1 Preheat the grill or smoker to 300 degrees.

2 Preheat the oven to 350 degrees.

3 Let the lamb sit out and reach room temperature.

4 Slather the lamb shanks with olive oil.

5 Rub the Steak Seasoning all over the shanks.

6 Place the shanks on the grill and sear the outside for about 10 minutes, until browned all around.

7 Remove the shanks and set aside.

8 To a large stovetop, ovenproof casserole dish with a lid, add the 2 teaspoons of olive oil, garlic, onions, and carrots and sauté over medium to low heat for approximately 5 minutes, until the onion is clear and the carrots are slightly soft.

9 Add the flour, Italian seasoning, and bay leaf, and stir together.

10 Add the tomato sauce, tomato paste, red wine, and beef stock and stir thoroughly.

11 Place the seared lamb shanks on top and cover.

12 Place the covered casserole dish in the oven for 2½ hours until the shanks are falling apart.

13 Remove from the oven and serve over mashed potatoes, rice, or pasta.

PER SERVING: *Calories 642 (From Fat 188); Fat 21g (Saturated 7g); Cholesterol 194mg; Sodium 1,902mg; Carbohydrate 27g (Dietary Fiber 4g); Protein 68g.*

Lamb Ribs

PREP TIME: 30 MIN	COOK TIME: 1–1½ HR	YIELD: 4 SERVINGS

INGREDIENTS

2 racks of lamb ribs, approximately 3 to 4 pounds

½ cup olive oil

½ cup Lamb Rub (see Chapter 12)

1 cup Basic BBQ Sauce (see Chapter 13 or use your favorite sauce)

DIRECTIONS

1 Preheat the grill or smoker to 250 degrees.

2 Let the lamb sit out and reach room temperature.

3 Slather the racks of ribs with the olive oil.

4 Rub the Lamb Rub on the ribs.

5 Place the ribs on the smoker over indirect heat.

6 Smoke the ribs until tender and an internal temperature of 180 degrees is reached.

7 Slather the ribs with barbecue sauce 5 minutes before you remove them from the smoker or grill.

8 Remove from the smoker.

9 Slice and serve hot.

PER SERVING: *Calories 663 (From Fat 489); Fat 54g (Saturated 15g); Cholesterol 91mg; Sodium 2,319mg; Carbohydrate 23g (Dietary Fiber 0g); Protein 20g.*

NOTE: Lamb ribs are smaller than pork ribs and cook much faster.

Stuffed Lamb Breast

PREP TIME: 30 MIN	COOK TIME: 45–90 MIN	YIELD: 4 SERVINGS

INGREDIENTS

1 boneless lamb breast

1 tablespoon olive oil plus enough to coat the lamb

¼ cup Lamb Rub (see Chapter 12)

2 tablespoons butter

½ cup diced celery (¼-inch dice)

½ cup minced yellow onion

1 tablespoon minced garlic

½ cup diced carrots (¼-inch dice)

3 cups Italian breadcrumbs

1 teaspoon sage

1 cup vegetable stock

1 egg yolk

Coarse ground salt to taste

Coarse ground pepper to taste

DIRECTIONS

1 Preheat the grill or smoker to 250 degrees.

2 Let the lamb sit out and reach room temperature.

3 Slather the breast on both sides with olive oil.

4 Rub the Lamb Rub all over the lamb breast.

5 To a sauté pan, add the butter and 1 tablespoon of olive oil and heat over low to medium heat.

6 Add the celery, onion, garlic, and carrots and sauté for 10 minutes, until the vegetables are softened.

7 Remove from the heat.

8 In a large mixing bowl, add the breadcrumbs, sage, and vegetable stock and mix.

9 Add the sautéed vegetable mixture and the egg yolk and mix thoroughly. Add the salt and pepper to taste.

10 Lay out the lamb breast and slather the mixture evenly over one side.

11 Roll the breast up with the mixture on the inside and tie with cotton kitchen twine.

12 Place the lamb on the smoker over indirect heat and smoke for 45 to 90 minutes, until the internal temperature reaches 125 degrees.

13 Move the rack to the direct-heat side of the grill and sear on all sides.

14 When the meat reaches an internal temperature of 145 degrees, remove it from the heat and let it rest for 10 minutes.

15 Cut away the twine, slice, and serve hot.

PER SERVING: *Calories 917 (From Fat 416); Fat 46g (Saturated 19g); Cholesterol 225mg; Sodium 3,113mg; Carbohydrate 67g (Dietary Fiber 5g); Protein 55g.*

TIP: You may not be familiar with lamb breast, but it's a value cut that has quite a lot of fat and can be tough if cooked incorrectly. Treat it as you would pork belly, and you're good to go. The layer of fat brings oodles of flavor and helps to tenderize the meat as it cooks.

Chapter **11**

Pork

P ork *is* barbecue in the south, and when you talk about barbecue in any region, pork is always part of the conversation. In Tennessee, where I'm from, pork is the first thing you think of when you hear the word *barbecue.* Today, the barbecue world has expanded beyond just pork, but make no mistake, if you want to cook barbecue, you'd better be able to smoke some pork.

In this chapter, I offer a range of recipes, from old staples to new standards. I give you recipes with large primals and with cuts you may have never seen before, such as a crown roast of pork. With a crown roast, you create the crown by tying the pork up into what looks like a crown. The bones are *frenched,* meaning trimmed down on the long, bone side to be bare.

If you really want to have great pork barbecue, you probably want it pulled. You achieve this by taking the pork up to an internal temperature of 192 degrees so that the fat and connective tissue breaks down and the meat pulls apart.

REMEMBER

At 160 degrees, the meat will *stall* (stop increasing in temperature) and may hold at 160 degrees for several hours. Relax — this is normal. Don't increase the temperature of your grill or smoker. Stay calm and keep smoking.

BBQ Pork Butt (Pulled Pork)

PREP TIME: ABOUT 10 MIN	COOK TIME: 12–16 HR	YIELD: 14 SERVINGS

INGREDIENTS

1 whole pork butt

½ cup kosher large-flake salt

1 cup Basic BBQ Rub (see Chapter 12)

2 cups Basic Mop Sauce (see Chapter 13)

DIRECTIONS

1 Preheat the grill or smoker to 220 degrees.

2 Unwrap the pork butt and rinse with cold water.

3 Trim the pork butt to leave ¼ inch of fat on the fatty areas.

4 Rub the butt uniformly with the salt.

5 Rub the butt uniformly with the Basic BBQ Rub.

6 Fill a spray bottle with the Basic Mop Sauce, and spritz the meat with it once an hour, making sure the meat gets thoroughly moistened.

7 Check the meat temperature after about 6 hours.

8 Remove your pork butt from the smoker when the internal temperature reaches 192 degrees. Allow it to rest on the counter or in a cooler for at least 1 hour before pulling and serving.

PER SERVING: *Calories 572 (From Fat 299); Fat 34g (Saturated 12g); Cholesterol 189mg; Sodium 1,617mg; Carbohydrate 3g (Dietary Fiber 0g); Protein 50g.*

Pork Belly Burnt Ends

PREP TIME: ABOUT 10 MIN | COOK TIME: 12–16 HR | YIELD: 10 SERVINGS

INGREDIENTS

1 whole skinless pork belly

2 tablespoons kosher large-flake salt

1 cup Basic BBQ Rub (see Chapter 12)

16 ounces Basic Mop Sauce (see Chapter 13)

½ cup stick butter sliced into ¼-inch slices

16 ounces Sweet Heat BBQ Sauce (see Chapter 13)

DIRECTIONS

1 Preheat the grill or smoker to 220 degrees.

2 Unwrap the pork belly and rinse with cold water.

3 Dice the belly into uniform 1-inch cubes and sprinkle with salt.

4 Rub the belly pieces uniformly with the Basic BBQ Rub.

5 Place the pieces on the smoker over indirect heat. *Note:* If the grates of your grill are so far apart that you fear the pork will fall through, use a grill basket or rack (see Chapter 3).

6 Fill a spray bottle with the Basic Mop Sauce, and spritz the meat once an hour, making sure the meat gets thoroughly moistened.

7 Smoke the pieces for 2½ hours at 220 degrees.

8 Remove the pieces from the heat and place them in a disposable aluminum pan.

9 Add the butter slices and Sweet Heat BBQ Sauce.

10 Cover with foil and seal tight.

11 Place the pan back on the smoker and smoke for another 90 minutes.

12 Remove the pan from the heat, let it rest 10 minutes, and serve hot.

PER SERVING: *Calories 1,521 (From Fat 1,124); Fat 125g (Saturated 44g); Cholesterol 271mg; Sodium 3,304mg; Carbohydrate 3g (Dietary Fiber 0g); Protein 73g.*

Porchetta

PREP TIME: 45 MIN | COOK TIME: 4–5 HR | YIELD: 12 SERVINGS

INGREDIENTS

1 whole skinless pork belly

2 tablespoons fennel seeds

1 tablespoon crushed red pepper flakes

¼ cup fresh or 4 teaspoons dried rosemary

¼ cup fresh or 4 teaspoons dried thyme

1 tablespoon coarse-ground black pepper

1 tablespoon kosher salt

¼ cup fresh garlic cloves

½ cup olive oil

DIRECTIONS

1 Preheat the grill or smoker to 220 degrees with the fire on one side.

2 Unwrap the pork belly, rinse with cold water, and set aside.

3 In a sauté pan, lightly toast the fennel seeds and red pepper flakes until you smell the aroma.

4 Place the toasted seeds and pepper flakes in a spice grinder, and grind into a powder.

5 Place the rosemary, thyme, olive oil, pepper, garlic, and ground spices in a food processor and pulse until thoroughly mixed.

6 Rub the belly uniformly with the kosher salt and then with the spice paste from the food processor, reserving ¼ cup of the spice paste.

7 Slather the spice paste uniformly on the interior of the belly (the side without the fat cap).

8 Roll up the belly and tie it with kitchen twine.

9 Rub the reserved spice paste on the exterior of the rolled belly.

10 Place the belly on the grill over indirect heat.

11 Check the meat temperature after about 3 hours.

12 When the meat reaches 150 degrees, move the porchetta from indirect heat over to the direct heat.

13 Sear and blister the outside of the belly, crisping up the fat on the outside.

14 Keep smoking until the internal temperature reaches 160 degrees.

15 Remove from the smoker and let rest for 30 minutes.

16 Slice and serve hot.

PER SERVING: *Calories 1,183 (From Fat 945); Fat 105g (Saturated 33g); Cholesterol 205mg; Sodium 1,877mg; Carbohydrate 2g (Dietary Fiber 1g); Protein 60g.*

Smoked Bacon

PREP TIME: 5 DAYS | COOK TIME: 3 HR | YIELD: 12 SERVINGS

INGREDIENTS

1 whole skinless pork belly

4 cups kosher large-flake salt

4 cups light brown sugar

1 cup coarse-ground black pepper

DIRECTIONS

1 Unwrap the pork belly and rinse with cold water; set aside.

2 In a large mixing bowl, mix the salt and brown sugar together thoroughly.

3 Thoroughly coat the belly on all sides with the salt-and-sugar mixture, making sure to cover every inch of the meat.

4 Place the coated meat back in the large bowl or on a sheet tray and cover with a lid or food wrap. If you have a rack and can elevate the meat, so much the better. A cooking rack on a sheet tray works great, too.

5 Refrigerate, checking the meat and turning it every day for 5 days. (This process removes the moisture and cures the meat.) Remove the liquid from the bottom of the bowl or tray every day.

6 After 5 days, remove the belly and rinse it thoroughly.

7 Coat the belly with the black pepper.

8 Preheat the grill or smoker to 200 degrees.

9 Put the belly in the smoker on indirect heat.

10 Smoke until an internal temperature of 160 degrees is reached.

11 Remove from the smoker and cool.

12 Store in the refrigerator or freezer until ready to serve.

13 Slice the bacon off the slab and fry for a delicious treat.

PER SERVING: *Calories 1,389 (From Fat 947); Fat 105g (Saturated 33g); Cholesterol 205mg; Sodium 19,534mg; Carbohydrate 55g (Dietary Fiber 3g); Protein 61g.*

Candied Grilled Bacon

PREP TIME: ABOUT 10 MIN	COOK TIME: 20–40 MINUTES	YIELD: 4 SERVINGS

INGREDIENTS

½ cup maple syrup

½ cup red-pepper jelly

1 pound thick-cut bacon

Fine-ground black pepper to taste

DIRECTIONS

1 Preheat the grill or smoker to 250 degrees.

2 In a bowl, mix the maple syrup and jelly to form a glaze.

3 Place the bacon on the grill over direct heat and cook almost to your desired doneness.

4 In the last 5 minutes, start basting the bacon with the glaze mixture.

5 Continue to glaze and turn the bacon every minute.

6 When the bacon is fully glazed (after 5 or 6 turns), sprinkle with the black pepper to taste.

7 Remove from the heat and place on a drying rack or cookie sheet to cool.

8 Serve warm.

PER SERVING: *Calories 669 (From Fat 332); Fat 37g (Saturated 12g); Cholesterol 91mg; Sodium 1,880mg; Carbohydrate 54g (Dietary Fiber 0g); Protein 30g.*

Dry Ribs

PREP TIME: ABOUT 20 MIN	COOK TIME: 3 HR	YIELD: 6 SERVINGS

INGREDIENTS

3 slabs loin back ribs (also known as baby back ribs)

1 tablespoon course-ground kosher salt

2 cups Basic Mop Sauce (see Chapter 13)

3 tablespoons dry seasoning (Peg Leg Porker Dry Rub, Rendezvous Famous Seasoning, or your favorite rub from Chapter 12)

DIRECTIONS

1 Preheat the grill or smoker to 250 degrees.

2 Unwrap the ribs and rinse with cold water.

3 Remove the membrane, or silver skin, from the ribs (see the Tip).

4 Sprinkle the ribs liberally with the salt.

5 Set the ribs on the smoker over indirect heat.

6 Fill a spray bottle with the Basic Mop Sauce and spritz the ribs every 30 minutes. (You can mop them with the Basic Mop Sauce instead, if you prefer.)

7 The ribs should be done after 3 to 3½ hours, but they may be done sooner, depending on their size. To check for doneness, run tongs under the ribs lengthwise to about the halfway point and lift. If the ribs sag like they're going to break, they're done.

8 Remove the ribs and mop one last time.

9 Dust with the dry seasoning and serve.

PER SERVING: *Calories 916 (From Fat 656); Fat 74g (Saturated 27g); Cholesterol 290mg; Sodium 969mg; Carbohydrate 4g (Dietary Fiber 0g); Protein 60g.*

TIP: The membrane is the skin on the back of the rib where you clearly see the white fat and bones. Use the handle of a spoon to get under the skin and then with a paper towel, grab it and pull it off the rib. If you can't get it, you can use a sharp knife to score it in a crisscross pattern and then remove it.

Wet Ribs

INGREDIENTS

3 slabs loin back ribs (also known as baby back ribs)

1 tablespoon coarse-ground kosher salt

1 cup Basic BBQ Rub (see Chapter 12)

2 cups Basic Mop Sauce (see Chapter 13)

2 cups Basic BBQ Sauce or Sweet Heat BBQ Sauce (see Chapter 13)

DIRECTIONS

1 Preheat the grill or smoker to 250 degrees.

2 Unwrap the ribs and rinse with cold water.

3 Turn the ribs over and remove the membrane (see the Tip).

4 Sprinkle the ribs liberally with the salt.

5 Rub the ribs with the Basic BBQ Rub.

6 Set the ribs on the smoker over indirect heat.

7 Fill a spray bottle with the Basic Mop Sauce and spritz the ribs every 30 minutes. (You can mop them with the Basic Mop Sauce instead, if you prefer.)

8 The ribs should be done after 3 to 3½ hours, but they may be done sooner, depending on their size. To check the ribs for doneness, run tongs under the ribs lengthwise to about the halfway point and lift. If the ribs sag like they're going to break, they're done.

9 Before the ribs are done (about the last 10 minutes), baste them with the Basic BBQ Sauce or Sweet Heat BBQ Sauce and get a good coating. Watch them closely so they don't burn.

10 Remove the ribs and serve.

PER SERVING: *Calories 1,078 (From Fat 774); Fat 74g (Saturated 27g); Cholesterol 290mg; Sodium 1,934mg; Carbohydrate 30g (Dietary Fiber 0g); Protein 60g.*

TIP: The membrane is the skin on the back of the rib. Use the handle of a spoon to get under the skin and then grab it with a paper towel and pull it off the rib. If you can't get it that way, use a sharp knife to score it in a crisscross pattern and then pull it off.

Fried Ribs

PREP TIME: ABOUT 15 MIN | COOK TIME: 4 MIN | YIELD: 6 SERVINGS

INGREDIENTS

1 smoked rack of dry ribs, chilled (see the Dry Ribs recipe in this chapter)

2 cups flour

¼ cup Basic BBQ Rub (see Chapter 12)

1 cup buttermilk

1 egg

1 quart vegetable oil

DIRECTIONS

1 Preheat the oil in a frying pan to 350 degrees.

2 In a shallow dish, thoroughly mix the flour and the Basic BBQ Rub.

3 In a separate dish, whisk the buttermilk and egg together thoroughly.

4 Cut the ribs into one-bone sections.

5 Dip each rib in the egg wash.

6 Dredge each rib in the flour mixture.

7 Fill a medium frying pan with the vegetable oil and heat to 350 degrees.

8 Deep-fry the ribs for 4 minutes or until golden brown.

9 Drain on paper towel or a drying rack and serve hot.

PER SERVING: *Calories 1,234 (From Fat 809); Fat 91g (Saturated 29g); Cholesterol 629mg; Sodium 2,099mg; Carbohydrate 38g (Dietary Fiber 1g); Protein 67g.*

Smoked Pork Loin

PREP TIME: ABOUT 10 MIN	COOK TIME: 45 MIN	YIELD: 10 SERVINGS

INGREDIENTS

1 pork loin at room temperature

1 cup yellow mustard

1 cup Basic BBQ Rub (see Chapter 12)

DIRECTIONS

1 Preheat the grill or smoker to 220 degrees with the fire on one side.

2 Rub the entire loin with the yellow mustard.

3 Rub the Basic BBQ Rub on top of the yellow mustard.

4 Place the loin on the smoker over indirect heat.

5 Check the temperature after 45 minutes.

6 When the meat reaches an internal temperature of 145 degrees, remove it from the smoker and let it rest for 30 minutes.

7 Slice and serve hot.

PER SERVING: *Calories 802 (From Fat 325); Fat 36g (Saturated 12g); Cholesterol 286mg; Sodium 931mg; Carbohydrate 10g (Dietary Fiber 3g); Protein 106g.*

Grilled Braised Pork Shank

| PREP TIME: 30 MIN | COOK TIME: 3 HR | YIELD: 4 SERVINGS |

INGREDIENTS

4 pork shanks at room temperature

2 teaspoons olive oil plus enough to coat the meat

½ cup Steak Seasoning (see Chapter 12)

¼ cup minced garlic

1 large white onion, diced

2 large carrots, peeled and cut into ½-inch rounds

¼ cup flour

2 cups tomato sauce

2 teaspoons tomato paste

1½ cups red wine of your choice

2 teaspoons Italian seasoning

1 bay leaf

2 cups beef stock

1 teaspoon coarsely ground salt

1 teaspoon coarsely ground black pepper

DIRECTIONS

1 Preheat the grill or smoker to 300 degrees.

2 Preheat the oven to 350 degrees.

3 Slather the shanks with olive oil.

4 Rub the Steak Seasoning all over the shanks.

5 Place the shanks on the grill and sear the outside until browned, about 10 minutes. Remove the shanks and set aside.

6 In a heatproof casserole dish, add the 2 teaspoons of olive oil, garlic, onion, and carrots, and sauté for approximately 5 minutes, until the onion becomes transparent and the carrots soften.

7 Add the flour and stir everything together.

8 Add the tomato sauce, tomato paste, red wine, Italian seasoning, bay leaf, and beef stock, and stir thoroughly.

9 Place the seared pork shanks on top and cover.

10 Braise in the oven for 2½ hours until the shanks are falling apart.

11 Remove from the oven and serve over mashed potatoes, rice, or pasta.

PER SERVING: *Calories 936 (From Fat 495); Fat 55g (Saturated 19g); Cholesterol 235mg; Sodium 1,917mg; Carbohydrate 21g (Dietary Fiber 2g); Protein 69g.*

Crown Roast of Pork

PREP TIME: 30 MIN	COOK TIME: 45–90 MIN	YIELD: 8 SERVINGS

INGREDIENTS

1 bone-in whole pork loin (ask your butcher to French the bones), at room temperature

1 tablespoon olive oil plus enough to coat the meat

½ cup Steak Seasoning (see Chapter 12)

2 tablespoons butter

½ cup diced celery (¼-inch dice)

½ cup minced yellow onion

1 tablespoon minced garlic

½ cup diced carrots (¼-inch dice)

3 cups Italian bread crumbs

1 cup vegetable stock

1 egg yolk

Salt to taste

Black pepper to taste

DIRECTIONS

1 Preheat the grill or smoker to 250 degrees.

2 Slather the loin on both sides with olive oil.

3 Rub the Steak Seasoning all over the loin.

4 In a sauté pan, heat the butter and 1 tablespoon of olive oil over medium heat until the butter melts.

5 Add the celery, onion, garlic, and carrots, and sauté for 10 minutes, until softened.

6 In a bowl, put the bread crumbs and vegetable stock and mix thoroughly.

7 Add the sautéed mixture and egg yolk, and mix thoroughly.

8 Add salt and pepper to taste.

9 Place the pork loin on a baking tray with the bones pointing up. Wrap it back on itself in the shape of a crown. Tie it in that shape with kitchen twine, doing a full loop around the roast.

10 Fill the interior of the roast with the stuffing mixture.

11 Place the roast on the smoker over indirect heat and smoke for 45 to 90 minutes, depending on size.

12 When the meat reaches an internal temperature of 145 degrees, remove it from the heat, and let it rest for 10 minutes.

13 Cut away the twine, slice, and serve hot.

PER SERVING: *Calories 830 (From Fat 324); Fat 37g (Saturated 12g); Cholesterol 236mg; Sodium 7,739mg; Carbohydrate 43g (Dietary Fiber 9g); Protein 80g.*

Carnitas Tacos

PREP TIME: ABOUT 10 MIN | **COOK TIME: 2 HR** | **YIELD: 8 SERVINGS**

INGREDIENTS

BBQ Pork Butt (see recipe earlier in this chapter)

2 cans flavorful local beer

2 tablespoons taco seasoning, plus more to taste

Eight 6-inch flour tortillas

1 cup diced onions

½ cup minced cilantro

DIRECTIONS

1 Preheat the oven to 300 degrees.

2 In a braising pan, add the whole pork butt, beer, and taco seasoning.

3 Cover the pot and braise the pork butt for 2 hours. After 2 hours, the pork should be completely falling apart.

4 Add more taco seasoning to taste.

5 To assemble the tacos, lay out the tortillas, place a small handful of pork on each, and then add the diced onion.

6 Add a sprinkle of the cilantro to each taco and serve flat.

PER SERVING: *Calories 717 (From Fat 320); Fat 36g (Saturated 13g); Cholesterol 189mg; Sodium 1,865mg; Carbohydrate 25g (Dietary Fiber 1g); Protein 53g.*

TIP: To *braise* is to cook slowly in fat and liquid in a covered pot.

BBQ Pizza

PREP TIME: ABOUT 10 MIN | COOK TIME: 10–20 MIN | YIELD: 8 SERVINGS

INGREDIENTS

1 cup Basic BBQ Sauce (see Chapter 13)

1 premade pizza crust

1 cup shredded mozzarella cheese

½ pound pulled pork barbecue (see BBQ Pork Butt recipe earlier in this chapter)

¼ cup sliced pickled jalapeño peppers

DIRECTIONS

1   Preheat the grill or smoker to 375 degrees.

2   Pour the Basic BBQ Sauce on the pizza crust and spread evenly in a circular pattern.

3   Sprinkle the mozzarella evenly over the sauce.

4   Spread the pulled pork evenly on the pizza.

5   Add the sliced jalapeños evenly around the pizza.

6   If you have a pizza stone, place the pizza on the stone over direct heat. If you don't have a pizza stone, place the pizza on the grate over indirect heat.

7   Cook for 10 to 20 minutes checking periodically for doneness.

PER SERVING: *Calories 288 (From Fat 76); Fat 9g (Saturated 3g); Cholesterol 33mg; Sodium 976mg; Carbohydrate 36g (Dietary Fiber 1g); Protein 14g.*

Glazed Ham

PREP TIME: ABOUT 10 MIN | **COOK TIME: 3 HR** | **YIELD: 10 SERVINGS**

INGREDIENTS

1 spiral-sliced ham

2 cups Dr Pepper Glaze (see Chapter 13), divided

DIRECTIONS

1 Preheat the grill or smoker to 220 degrees.

2 Open the spiral-sliced ham and put it flat side down on a baking dish.

3 Glaze the ham with the Dr Pepper Glaze by applying it with a basting brush. Use about ¼ cup each time you glaze.

4 Place the glazed ham on the smoker on indirect heat.

5 Glaze thoroughly every 30 minutes. Repeat until you feel it has enough glaze. *Remember:* This ham is already cooked so you're just warming and glazing it.

PER SERVING: *Calories 565 (From Fat 258); Fat 29g (Saturated 10g); Cholesterol 187mg; Sodium 4,773mg; Carbohydrate 12g (Dietary Fiber 0g); Protein 72g.*

Whole Hog

INGREDIENTS

One 100- to 150-pound whole hog

2 cups coarse-ground salt

1 gallon Basic Mop Sauce (see Chapter 13)

1 rick hickory wood

DIRECTIONS

1   In a charcoal chimney and in the bottom of a barbecue pit, start a fire. You use the chimney-started fire to create coals to shovel under the hog during the cook and the fire in the pit to get the cooking fire going.

2   When the wood has burned down to coals, move it to the corners of the pit.

3   Place an oven thermometer in each corner of the pit. Wipe a little bit of cooking oil on the surface so that when the thermometer smokes up, you can wipe the face to clear away the smoke and read the temperature. Ideally, the temperature in the pit should be between 200 and 220 degrees. If the temperature reaches 250 degrees, you're still okay, but you don't want it any higher than 250 degrees.

4   To prep the hog, lay it on its back. Generally, the butcher splits the hog, but you'll need help from some friends to pull the rib cage outward. Then use a hatchet and hammer to split the spine on the inner cavity of the hog. Split it all the way down from head to tail. Be careful not to go through the spine — just split it enough that the hog will lay down flat on its back.

5   When the hog is laying somewhat flat on its back, pull the membrane away from the rib cage and clean up any unsightly areas. Remove any large pockets of fat. (More than likely the butcher has already removed the organs, but sometimes the kidneys are left. If there are organs, remove them.)

(continued)

6   Rub the salt completely and liberally over the interior cavity of the hog.

7   Lay the hog in the pit, belly side down, on a cooking grate.

8   Maintain the fire at 220 degrees by adding hot coals to the corners of the pit about every hour.

9   At about 6 hours, carefully flip the hog onto its back.

10   Maintain the fire by adding hot coals and start mopping the hog every hour with Basic Mop Sauce until the internal temperature reaches 192 degrees. Check the temperature in both the shoulders and the hams.

11   When the hog is done, let it rest for 30 minutes; then pull the meat from the bones. While pulling, you separate the fat and bones from the edible meat. The fat should be rendered enough to make this a fairly easy process. If any pieces of meat are still tough, you can chop them into smaller bites.

VARY IT! For added flavor, coat the inner cavity with 2 cups Basic BBQ Rub (see Chapter 12) after you flip the hog onto its back.

TIP: Unless you have a really big smoker, check Chapter 4 for information on how to build a pit to smoke the whole pig.

PER SERVING: *Calories 468 (From Fat 248); Fat 28g (Saturated 10g); Cholesterol 160mg; Sodium 1,579mg; Carbohydrate 0g (Dietary Fiber 0g); Protein 51g.*

4

Sides, Sauces, and Then Some

Build the perfect rub, and the perfect brine, and the perfect marinade. Assemble liquid brines and marinades and soak meat in them before you cook it. Or mix seasonings together and rub them on the meat before you put it on the grate — or do both!

Mix up a great barbecue sauce. You can go tangy or sweet, start with a tomato base or vinegar or even mustard, and adjust to suit your taste.

Start your barbecue feast with an appetizer. After all, the meat cooks for a while, so you have time to enjoy a dip, some salad, or a veggie hors d'oeuvre.

Cook up accompaniments for the main attraction. Beans and coleslaw are traditional barbecue side dishes, and you get recipes for a few varieties of each. You can branch out to roasted vegetables and several types of salad.

Finish off your meal with a sweet treat. End your barbecue feast with some fruit — grilled or fresh — bake a cake, make a pie, or enjoy banana pudding or bananas Foster. A great barbecue meal deserves a great finish!

Chapter **12**

Rubs, Brines, and Marinades

n this chapter, I offer up recipes for rubs, brines, and marinades. All three are essential to barbecue, but they're used in very different ways:

» **Rubs:** A *rub* is a dry seasoning blend you typically rub on meat before cooking. In some instances, you rub the meat down many hours before the cook so that it becomes almost a dry brine. Most often, you add it just before you start cooking. In some cases, you add the rub at the end of the cook. It all depends on the effect you want on your meat. Leaving a rub on for hours before the cook changes the flavor of the meat itself. Putting on the rub just before you cook flavors the surface most noticeably while still altering the meat slightly. Putting it on at the end of the cook results in almost all surface flavor, letting the natural flavor of the meat shine through.

>> **Brines:** A *brine* is a saltwater solution that penetrates the structure of the meat through *osmosis* — a scientific way of saying that it seeps in. Because a brine penetrates the meat's cell wall, it alters and enhances the meat's flavor. You need to give a brine time to work, usually a couple of hours if not overnight. The exception is seafood, which can be brined although it isn't done often. If you brine fish, use a simple saltwater brine and cook it immediately.

>> **Marinades:** A *marinade* is a sauce meant to help enhance the flavor of your meat but not fully penetrate it as a brine does. Marinades are not always water soluble — they're typically oil based, so they tend to alter just the surface of the meat. You place meat and vegetables in a marinade for 2 to 4 hours to soak before you put the food on the grill. You can also use a marinade as a baste during the cook.

Basic BBQ Rub (Pork Rub)

PREP TIME: ABOUT 10 MIN	COOK TIME: NONE	YIELD: 6 SERVINGS

INGREDIENTS

½ cup paprika

¼ cup chili powder

1 tablespoon coarse ground black pepper

1 tablespoon coarse ground kosher salt

¼ cup brown sugar

1 teaspoon onion powder

1 tablespoon garlic powder

1 teaspoon ground allspice

DIRECTIONS

1 In a large mixing bowl, add all the ingredients and mix thoroughly.

2 Store in a sealed container in a cool, dark space.

PER SERVING: *Calories 77 (From Fat 18); Fat 2g (Saturated 0g); Cholesterol 0mg; Sodium 616mg; Carbohydrate 17g (Dietary Fiber 5g); Protein 2g.*

Brisket Rub

PREP TIME: ABOUT 10 MIN | COOK TIME: NONE | YIELD: 6 SERVINGS

INGREDIENTS

½ cup coarse ground black pepper

½ cup coarse ground kosher salt

¼ cup brown sugar

¼ cup minced garlic

1 teaspoon ground allspice

DIRECTIONS

1 In a large mixing bowl, add all the ingredients and mix thoroughly.

2 Store in a sealed container in a cool, dark space.

PER SERVING: *Calories 43 (From Fat 0); Fat 0g (Saturated 0g); Cholesterol 0mg; Sodium 4,484mg; Carbohydrate 11g (Dietary Fiber 0g); Protein 0g.*

Chicken Rub

INGREDIENTS

½ cup garlic salt

1 tablespoon coarse ground black pepper

1 teaspoon onion powder

½ teaspoon rubbed sage

DIRECTIONS

1 In a large mixing bowl, add all the ingredients and mix thoroughly.

2 Store in a sealed container in a cool, dark space.

PER SERVING: *Calories 2 (From Fat 0); Fat 0g (Saturated 0g); Cholesterol 0mg; Sodium 7,840mg; Carbohydrate 0g (Dietary Fiber 0g); Protein 0g.*

Lamb Rub

INGREDIENTS

¼ cup minced garlic

¼ cup coarse ground black pepper

¼ cup coarse ground kosher salt

¼ cup dried rosemary or ¾ cup fresh rosemary

¼ cup dried thyme or ¾ cup fresh thyme

1 teaspoon dry mustard powder

DIRECTIONS

1 In a large mixing bowl, add all the ingredients and mix thoroughly.

2 Store in a sealed container in a cool, dark space.

PER SERVING: *Calories 35 (From Fat 6); Fat 1g (Saturated 0g); Cholesterol 0mg; Sodium 2,246mg; Carbohydrate 8g (Dietary Fiber 3g); Protein 1g.*

Salt and Pepper Rub

PREP TIME: ABOUT 10 MIN	COOK TIME: NONE	YIELD: 6 SERVINGS

INGREDIENTS

3 cups course ground black pepper

1 cup kosher salt

DIRECTIONS

1 In a large mixing bowl, add all the ingredients and mix thoroughly.

2 Store in a sealed container in a cool, dark space.

PER SERVING: *Calories 131 (From Fat 15); Fat 2g (Saturated 1g); Cholesterol 0mg; Sodium 8,983mg; Carbohydrate 33g (Dietary Fiber 14g); Protein 6g.*

Steak Seasoning

PREP TIME: ABOUT 10 MIN	COOK TIME: NONE	YIELD: 6 SERVINGS

INGREDIENTS

¼ cup coarse ground kosher salt

¼ cup coarse ground black pepper

¼ cup dried rosemary

¼ cup dried thyme

DIRECTIONS

1 In a large mixing bowl, add all the ingredients and mix thoroughly.

2 Store in a sealed container in a cool, dark space.

PER SERVING: *Calories 15 (From Fat 5); Fat 1g (Saturated 0g); Cholesterol 0mg; Sodium 2,243mg; Carbohydrate 3g (Dietary Fiber 2g); Protein 0g.*

Poultry Brine

| PREP TIME: ABOUT 20 MIN | COOK TIME: 20 MIN | YIELD: 10 SERVINGS |

INGREDIENTS

2 gallons water

4 bay leaves

½ cup black peppercorns

2 oranges, quartered

2 cups coarse ground salt

DIRECTIONS

1   In a stock pot, add all the ingredients and stir on low heat until all the salt is dissolved, about 20 minutes.

2   Let cool and then transfer to a 5-gallon bucket.

3   Refrigerate until ready to use, up to 2 days.

PER SERVING: *Calories 21 (From Fat 3); Fat 0g (Saturated 0g); Cholesterol 0mg; Sodium 10,755mg; Carbohydrate 10g (Dietary Fiber 3g); Protein 1g.*

NOTE: When you're ready to use the brine, submerse a bird in it and refrigerate or place in a cooler surrounded by ice and let it brine for at least 6 hours and up to 24 hours.

Pork Chop Brine

PREP TIME: ABOUT 20 MIN | COOK TIME: 20 MIN | YIELD: 4 SERVINGS

INGREDIENTS

½ gallon water

1 bay leaf

1 teaspoon black peppercorns

¼ cup maple syrup

½ cups coarse ground salt

1 sprig fresh thyme or
1 tablespoon dried thyme

DIRECTIONS

1 In a stock pot, add all the ingredients and stir on low heat until all the salt is dissolved, about 20 minutes.

2 Let cool and then transfer to a resealable bag.

3 Store in the refrigerator until ready to use, up to 2 days.

PER SERVING: *Calories 55 (From Fat 1); Fat 0g (Saturated 0g); Cholesterol 0mg; Sodium 6,723mg; Carbohydrate 15g (Dietary Fiber 1g); Protein 0g.*

NOTE: When you're ready to use the brine, place four 8-ounce pork chops in the resealable bag and let them brine in the refrigerator for at least 2 hours and up to 6 hours.

Sweet Tea Brine

PREP TIME: ABOUT 20 MIN | COOK TIME: 20 MIN | YIELD: 10 SERVINGS

INGREDIENTS

½ gallon sweet tea

1 bay leaf

1 teaspoon black peppercorns

¼ cup coarse ground salt

1 sprig rosemary or
1 tablespoon dried rosemary

2 garlic cloves, peeled

DIRECTIONS

1 In a stock pot, add all the ingredients and stir on low heat until all the salt is dissolved, about 20 minutes.

2 Let cool and then transfer to a resealable bag.

3 Refrigerate until ready to use, up to 2 days.

PER SERVING: *Calories 40 (From Fat 1); Fat 0g (Saturated 0g); Cholesterol 0mg; Sodium 1,350mg; Carbohydrate 11g (Dietary Fiber 0g); Protein 0g.*

NOTE: When you're ready to use the brine, place 2 pounds of the meat of your choice in the resealable bag and let it brine in the refrigerator for at least 2 hours and up to 6 hours.

Steak Marinade

PREP TIME: ABOUT 10 MIN | COOK TIME: NONE | YIELD: 6 SERVINGS

INGREDIENTS

⅓ cup olive oil

¼ cup soy sauce

¼ cup Worcestershire sauce

1 tablespoon lemon juice

1 teaspoon garlic powder or
3 teaspoons fresh minced
garlic

1 teaspoon black pepper

1 teaspoon dried parsley flakes

DIRECTIONS

1 In a medium mixing bowl, add all the ingredients and whisk thoroughly.

2 Transfer to a resealable bag.

3 Refrigerate until ready to use, up to 2 days.

PER SERVING: *Calories 113 (From Fat 97); Fat 11g (Saturated 1g); Cholesterol 0mg; Sodium 783mg; Carbohydrate 3g (Dietary Fiber 2g); Protein 1g.*

NOTE: When you're ready to use the marinade, place the steak in the resealable bag and let it marinate in the refrigerator for at least 2 hours.

Hawaiian Marinade

PREP TIME: ABOUT 10 MIN | COOK TIME: NONE | YIELD: 6 SERVINGS

INGREDIENTS

½ cup soy sauce

½ cup brown sugar

½ cup pineapple juice

1 tablespoon lemon juice

DIRECTIONS

1 In a medium mixing bowl, add all the ingredients and whisk until the sugar is dissolved.

2 Transfer to a resealable bag.

3 Refrigerate until ready to use, up to 2 days.

PER SERVING: *Calories 96 (From Fat 0); Fat 0g (Saturated 0g); Cholesterol 0mg; Sodium 1,346mg; Carbohydrate 22g (Dietary Fiber 0g); Protein 3g.*

NOTE: When you're ready to use the marinade, place the meat in the resealable bag and let it marinate in the refrigerator for at least 2 hours, but preferably 8 hours.

Chicken Marinade

PREP TIME: ABOUT 20 MIN	COOK TIME: NONE	YIELD: 10 SERVINGS

INGREDIENTS

10 ounces water

10 ounces apple cider vinegar

10 ounces apple juice

2 tablespoons lemon juice

1 tablespoon cracked black pepper

¼ cup Basic BBQ Rub (Pork Rub) (see recipe earlier in this chapter)

1 tablespoon vegetable oil

DIRECTIONS

1 In a medium mixing bowl, add all the ingredients and whisk thoroughly.

2 Transfer to a resealable bag.

PER SERVING: *Calories 92 (From Fat 21); Fat 2g (Saturated 0g); Cholesterol 0mg; Sodium 739mg; Carbohydrate 20g (Dietary Fiber 6g); Protein 2g.*

NOTE: When you're ready to use the marinade, place the meat in the resealable bag and let it marinate in the refrigerator for at least 2 hours.

Chapter **13**

Sauces

S ome people like sauce with their barbecue; some people don't. It all depends on taste. In Texas, they aren't big on sauce and want the meat to stand on its own. In Kansas City, sauce is boss. Other areas such as Memphis and North Carolina can go either way, but one thing is for sure: If you're going to have a sauce, you need a good one!

The recipes in this chapter give you basics for a wide variety of sauces.

Basic BBQ Sauce

PREP TIME: ABOUT 20 MIN	COOK TIME: NONE	YIELD: 10 SERVINGS

INGREDIENTS

2 cups ketchup

¼ cup honey

¼ cup brown sugar

⅛ cup yellow mustard

¼ cup apple cider vinegar

DIRECTIONS

1 In a large mixing bowl, add all the ingredients; whisk thoroughly.

2 Serve on your favorite barbecued pork, chicken, or beef.

PER SERVING: *Calories 90 (From Fat 3); Fat 0g (Saturated 0g); Cholesterol 0mg; Sodium 573mg; Carbohydrate 23g (Dietary Fiber 0g); Protein 1g.*

VARY IT! For an extra kick, add a teaspoon of your favorite barbecue seasoning or rub.

Mustard BBQ Sauce

INGREDIENTS

2 cups yellow mustard

½ cup apple cider vinegar

¼ cup honey

¼ cup brown sugar

1 teaspoon cayenne pepper

DIRECTIONS

1 In a saucepan, add all the ingredients.

2 Cook on low heat for 20 minutes, whisking thoroughly.

3 Serve on your favorite barbecued pork, chicken, or beef.

PER SERVING: *Calories 75 (From Fat 18); Fat 2g (Saturated 0g); Cholesterol 0mg; Sodium 567mg; Carbohydrate 13g (Dietary Fiber 2g); Protein 2g.*

VARY IT! For an extra kick, add a teaspoon of your favorite barbecue seasoning or rub.

Basic Mop Sauce

PREP TIME: ABOUT 20 MIN	COOK TIME: NONE	YIELD: 10 SERVINGS

INGREDIENTS

1⅓ cups water

1⅓ cups apple cider vinegar

1¼ cups apple juice

1 tablespoon Basic BBQ Rub (Pork Rub) (see Chapter 12)

1 tablespoon vegetable oil

DIRECTIONS

1 In a 1-quart mason jar, add all the ingredients.

2 Put the lid on the mason jar and shake vigorously.

3 Use as a baste or marinade on any meat.

PER SERVING: *Calories 49 (From Fat 13); Fat 2g (Saturated 0g); Cholesterol 2mg; Sodium 462mg; Carbohydrate 8g (Dietary Fiber 0g); Protein 0g.*

TIP: If you don't have a 1-quart mason jar, you can use any container with a screw-on lid as long as it's large enough to hold all the ingredients.

Alabama White Sauce

PREP TIME: ABOUT 20 MIN	COOK TIME: NONE	YIELD: 10 SERVINGS

INGREDIENTS

2 cups mayonnaise

¼ cup white vinegar

1 teaspoon coarse ground black pepper

¼ cup white sugar

Dash of Peg Leg Porker Dry Seasoning or Basic BBQ Rub (see Chapter 12)

DIRECTIONS

1 In a large mixing bowl, add the mayonnaise, vinegar, pepper, and sugar; whisk thoroughly. If the consistency is too thick, add more vinegar.

2 Add the seasoning, mix thoroughly, and refrigerate for at least 1 hour.

3 Use on your favorite poultry dishes.

PER SERVING: *Calories 204 (From Fat 141); Fat 16g (Saturated 2g); Cholesterol 12mg; Sodium 334mg; Carbohydrate 16g (Dietary Fiber 0g); Protein 0g.*

VARY IT! For a little more zest, add a little lemon juice or a tad of prepared horseradish.

Sweet Heat BBQ Sauce

PREP TIME: ABOUT 20 MIN	COOK TIME: NONE	YIELD: 10 SERVINGS

INGREDIENTS

2 cups ketchup

¼ cup honey

¼ cup brown sugar

⅛ cup yellow mustard

¼ cup apple cider vinegar

½ teaspoon of cayenne pepper

½ cup red pepper jelly

DIRECTIONS

1 In a large mixing bowl, add all the ingredients; whisk thoroughly.

2 Serve on your favorite barbecued pork, chicken, seafood, or beef.

PER SERVING: *Calories 130 (From Fat 3); Fat 0g (Saturated 0g); Cholesterol 0mg; Sodium 578mg; Carbohydrate 33g (Dietary Fiber 0g); Protein 1g.*

VARY IT! For an extra kick, add 1 teaspoon of your favorite barbecue seasoning or rub.

Vinegar BBQ Sauce

PREP TIME: ABOUT 20 MIN | COOK TIME: NONE | YIELD: 6 SERVINGS

INGREDIENTS

4 cups apple cider vinegar

½ cup hot sauce

¼ cup red pepper flakes

¼ cup sugar

Salt and pepper to taste

DIRECTIONS

1 In a large mixing bowl, add the vinegar, hot sauce, red pepper flakes, and sugar; mix thoroughly.

2 Add the salt and pepper.

3 Refrigerate for about an hour to meld the flavors.

PER SERVING: *Calories 70 (From Fat 2); Fat 0g (Saturated 0g); Cholesterol 0mg; Sodium 505mg; Carbohydrate 11g (Dietary Fiber 0g); Protein 0g.*

TIP: Use on a whole hog barbecue or a Carolina-style sandwich.

Rib Glaze

PREP TIME: ABOUT 20 MIN | COOK TIME: 30 MIN | YIELD: 6 SERVINGS

INGREDIENTS

4 tablespoons butter

¼ cup Basic BBQ Sauce (see Chapter 12)

2 cups red pepper jelly

¼ cup apple cider vinegar

DIRECTIONS

1 In a medium saucepan, melt the butter.

2 Add the remaining ingredients and heat on medium to high heat while stirring constantly.

3 Reduce down to a glaze consistency — when you pull the spoon out, it should be lightly coated.

4 Use as a glaze for ribs.

PER SERVING: *Calories 320 (From Fat 87); Fat 10g (Saturated 5g); Cholesterol 20mg; Sodium 689mg; Carbohydrate 63g (Dietary Fiber 6g); Protein 2g.*

TIP: If you use this glaze when grilling, be careful to add it late in the process. Because of the sugar, it can and will burn.

Chimichurri

INGREDIENTS

3 cups olive oil

2 cups red wine vinegar

4 bunches flat-leaf (Italian) parsley

2 bunches cilantro

1 cup peeled garlic cloves

1 ounce coarse ground salt

2 ounces coarse ground pepper

2 ounces red pepper flakes

DIRECTIONS

1　In the bowl of a food process, add the olive oil, vinegar, parsley, cilantro, garlic, salt, pepper, and red pepper flakes; pulse to blend the ingredients.

2　Remove from the food processor and refrigerate for several hours.

3　Use as a condiment for cooked meats or as a marinade for raw meats.

PER SERVING: *Calories 417 (From Fat 382); Fat 42g (Saturated 6g); Cholesterol 0mg; Sodium 700mg; Carbohydrate 11g (Dietary Fiber 2g); Protein 2g.*

NOTE: You can use the sauce immediately, but it's better if it chills for a few hours first.

Comeback Sauce

PREP TIME: ABOUT 20 MIN | COOK TIME: NONE | YIELD: 8 SERVINGS

INGREDIENTS

2 cups mayonnaise

½ cup ketchup

2 tablespoons hot sauce

1 tablespoons Worcestershire sauce

2 tablespoons honey

DIRECTIONS

1 In a large mixing bowl, add all the ingredients; whisk thoroughly.

2 Use on vegetables, fries, burgers, or anything else you want to jazz up!

PER SERVING: *Calories 427 (From Fat 394); Fat 44g (Saturated 5g); Cholesterol 32mg; Sodium 594mg; Carbohydrate 10g (Dietary Fiber 0g); Protein 1g.*

Whiskey Glaze

PREP TIME: ABOUT 20 MIN	COOK TIME: 20 MIN	YIELD: 6 SERVINGS

INGREDIENTS

1 cup peach preserves

½ cup brown sugar

½ cup honey

¼ cup apple cider vinegar

¼ cup whiskey

DIRECTIONS

1 In a medium saucepan, add the preserves, brown sugar, honey, and vinegar.

2 Heat on medium to high heat while constantly stirring until the sugar dissolves, about 20 minutes.

3 Add the whiskey, and stir in thoroughly.

4 Reduce down to a glaze consistency — when you pull out the spoon, it should be lightly coated.

5 Use as a glaze for a ham, ribs, or salmon.

PER SERVING: *Calories 286 (From Fat 1); Fat 0g (Saturated 0g); Cholesterol 0mg; Sodium 26mg; Carbohydrate 70g (Dietary Fiber 0g); Protein 0g.*

TIP: If you use this glaze when grilling, be careful to add it late in the process. Because of the sugar, it can and will burn.

Dr Pepper Glaze

PREP TIME: ABOUT 10 MIN | COOK TIME: 30 MIN | YIELD: 6 SERVINGS

INGREDIENTS

12 ounces Dr Pepper

½ cup brown sugar

¼ cup orange juice

1 teaspoon Dijon mustard

DIRECTIONS

1 In a medium saucepan, add all the ingredients.

2 Heat on medium to high heat, stirring constantly.

3 Reduce down to a glaze consistency — when you pull the spoon out, it should be lightly coated.

4 Use as a glaze for a ham, ribs, or salmon.

PER SERVING: *Calories 74 (From Fat 0); Fat 0g (Saturated 0g); Cholesterol 0mg; Sodium 16mg; Carbohydrate 19g (Dietary Fiber 0g); Protein 0g.*

TIP: If you use this glaze when grilling, be careful to add it late in the process. Because of the sugar, it can and will burn.

Mtn Dew White Sauce

PREP TIME: ABOUT 20 MIN	COOK TIME: 30 MIN	YIELD: 10 SERVINGS

INGREDIENTS

3 cups Mtn Dew

2 cups mayonnaise

¼ cup white vinegar

1 teaspoon coarse-ground black pepper

A dash Peg Leg Porker Dry Seasoning or seasoning of your choice (see Chapter 12)

DIRECTIONS

1 In a saucepan, add the Mtn Dew.

2 Cook on medium heat, stirring constantly, to reduce the Mtn Dew to a syrup-like consistency.

3 Transfer the Mtn Dew to a large mixing bowl. Add the mayonnaise, vinegar, and black pepper; whisk thoroughly. If the consistency is too thick, add more vinegar.

4 Add the seasoning and refrigerate for at least 1 hour.

5 Use on your favorite poultry dishes.

PER SERVING: Calories 215 (From Fat 141); Fat 16g (Saturated 2g); Cholesterol 12mg; Sodium 342mg; Carbohydrate 19g (Dietary Fiber 0g); Protein 1g.

VARY IT! Add a little lemon juice or a tad of prepared horseradish for an extra kick.

Chapter **14**

Appetizers

Smoking meat takes a long time, so you may want to offer some snacks or appetizers while the barbecue cooks. In this chapter, I offer some creative appetizer ideas to keep your guests satisfied before their big meal.

Stuffed Jalapeños

PREP TIME: 30 MIN | COOK TIME: 1 HR | YIELD: 12 SERVINGS

INGREDIENTS

6 whole fresh jalapeño peppers

1 cup cream cheese

1 cup pimento cheese

6 strips thinly sliced bacon

DIRECTIONS

1 Preheat the grill or smoker to 250 degrees.

2 Slice the jalapeños in half lengthwise.

3 With a spoon, scoop out the inner pulp and seeds of the peppers, leaving 12 hollow shells. Set aside.

4 In a bowl, combine the cream cheese and pimento cheese, and mix thoroughly.

5 Use a spatula to fill each jalapeño shell with the cheese mixture.

6 Cut the bacon strips in half.

7 Starting at the end of each pepper, and working diagonally, wrap one-half strip of bacon around each jalapeño. Stretch the bacon as you go so that it covers the jalapeño completely. The stretched bacon will stick to the pepper without needing a toothpick.

8 Place the jalapeños on the indirect heat side of the grill, open side up.

9 Smoke until the bacon is crisp. The bacon forms a shell around the peppers to keep the cheese from melting out.

10 Serve hot.

PER SERVING: *Calories 184 (From Fat 136); Fat 15g (Saturated 6g); Cholesterol 46mg; Sodium 578mg; Carbohydrate 5g (Dietary Fiber 0g); Protein 5g.*

Pimento Cheese

PREP TIME: ABOUT 20 MIN PLUS 30 MIN FOR REFRIGERATING	COOK TIME: NONE	YIELD: 12 SERVINGS

INGREDIENTS

One 4-ounce jar pimentos

¼ cup pickle juice

1 heaping tablespoon Miracle Whip, or to taste

16 ounces freshly grated cheddar cheese

Coarse-ground salt to taste

Coarse-ground pepper to taste

DIRECTIONS

1 In a food processor, place the pimentos with their juice, pickle juice, Miracle Whip, and cheddar cheese; pulse to blend together,

2 Add the salt and pepper.

3 If needed, add more Miracle Whip. The cheese mixture is supposed to be dense, so don't add more unless you want it to be creamier.

4 Remove from the food processor and chill for 30 minutes.

5 Serve cold spread on crackers.

PER SERVING: Calories 162 (From Fat 119); Fat 13g (Saturated 8g); Cholesterol 40mg; Sodium 719mg; Carbohydrate 1g (Dietary Fiber 0g); Protein 10g.

Jalapeño Silver-Dollar Corn Cakes

PREP TIME: ABOUT 20 MIN | COOK TIME: 3 MIN | YIELD: 6 SERVINGS

INGREDIENTS

1 cup self-rising flour

1 cup self-rising cornmeal mix

½ cup minced canned jalapeños

1 tablespoon jalapeño juice

1 tablespoon sugar

¼ teaspoon salt

¾ cup buttermilk

2 large eggs

½ cup water

¼ cup vegetable oil, plus enough to coat a griddle

¼ cup melted butter

DIRECTIONS

1 Preheat a griddle to medium high so that it's slightly smoking.

2 In a bowl, add all the ingredients except the melted butter; mix thoroughly. The batter should be the consistency of pancake batter.

3 Brush the griddle with vegetable oil to coat the surface.

4 With a large spoon, dollop the batter onto the griddle. The cakes should be about 2 inches in diameter.

5 As the batter starts to bubble and you can see bubbles all over the corn cakes, flip the cakes.

6 Cook until the cakes are golden brown and crispy, approximately 1 minute per side.

7 Serve hot with melted butter either drizzled on top or as a dipping sauce.

PER SERVING: *Calories 338 (From Fat 177); Fat 20g (Saturated 6g); Cholesterol 92mg; Sodium 683mg; Carbohydrate 34g (Dietary Fiber 2g); Protein 7g.*

Grilled Asparagus

PREP TIME: ABOUT 5 MIN | COOK TIME: 15 MIN | YIELD: 6 SERVINGS

INGREDIENTS

1 bunch asparagus

One 8-ounce bottle zesty Italian dressing

DIRECTIONS

1 Preheat the grill or smoker to 250 degrees.

2 In one hand, hold each asparagus spear by the stem. Gently bend the asparagus with your other hand. It should break a little above the base. Repeat with the remaining pieces of asparagus. Discard the tough stems.

3 In an ovenproof dish, place the asparagus and coat with the Italian dressing, making sure that all the pieces are thoroughly coated.

4 Place the coated asparagus on the grill and cook for about 15 minutes, until it's slightly charred and starts to bend when lifted.

5 Remove from the grill and place back in the dish with the dressing.

6 Serve hot.

PER SERVING: *Calories 120 (From Fat 100); Fat 11g (Saturated 2g); Cholesterol 0mg; Sodium 648mg; Carbohydrate 5g (Dietary Fiber 1g); Protein 1g.*

Chargrilled Oysters

PREP TIME: ABOUT 20 MIN | **COOK TIME: 20 MIN** | **YIELD: 12 SERVINGS**

INGREDIENTS

1 box rock salt

16 ounces (2 sticks) salted butter

½ cup minced garlic

½ cup minced chives

12 oysters

Juice of 1 lemon

Parsley flakes, for garnish

DIRECTIONS

1 Preheat the grill to 250 degrees.

2 On a baking sheet, spread the rock salt evenly. Set aside.

3 To a food processor or mixing bowl, add the butter, garlic, and chives. Blend thoroughly and set aside.

4 Shuck the oysters and place them on the baking sheet in the rock salt, shell side down. The texture of the salt holds the oysters' odd shape without spilling the contents.

5 Pour the lemon juice over the oysters.

6 Place the oysters on the indirect heat side of the grill.

7 Add wood chips to the grill, and let the oysters smoke for 5 minutes.

8 Add a spoonful of the butter mixture to each oyster.

9 Move the baking sheet over direct heat and broil for 5 minutes.

10 Remove from the heat when the oysters are sizzling.

11 Sprinkle with parsley flakes, and serve sizzling hot.

PER SERVING: *Calories 153 (From Fat 141); Fat 16g (Saturated 10g); Cholesterol 48mg; Sodium 139mg; Carbohydrate 2g (Dietary Fiber 0g); Protein 2g.*

NOTE: You don't consume the rock salt; it simply helps the oysters stay upright on a baking pan.

Smoked Catfish Dip

PREP TIME: ABOUT 20 MIN | **COOK TIME: 1 HR** | **YIELD: 6 SERVINGS**

INGREDIENTS

Two 8-ounce catfish filets

½ cup cream cheese, softened

½ cup sour cream

1 teaspoon minced shallots or minced red onion

Juice of half a lemon

Coarse ground salt to taste

Coarse ground pepper to taste

¼ cup fresh or 1 tablespoon dried chives

Minced parsley, for garnish

DIRECTIONS

1 Preheat the grill or smoker to 220 degrees.

2 Put the filets on indirect heat and smoke for approximately 1 hour. Smoke the catfish until it's flakey but not dry.

3 Remove from the heat and refrigerate for 10 minutes.

4 To a large bowl, add the cream cheese, sour cream, shallots or onion, and lemon juice; mix thoroughly.

5 Add the salt and pepper.

6 Break up the catfish into small chunks and fold it and the chives into the cream cheese mixture; mix thoroughly.

7 Place in a serving bowl and sprinkle with the parsley.

8 Serve cold with crackers.

PER SERVING: *Calories 163 (From Fat 108); Fat 12g (Saturated 6g); Cholesterol 72mg; Sodium 106mg; Carbohydrate 1g (Dietary Fiber 0g); Protein 12g.*

BBQ Skillet Nachos

PREP TIME: ABOUT 20 MIN	COOK TIME: 30 MIN	YIELD: 6 SERVINGS

INGREDIENTS

One 11-ounce bag corn tortilla chips

8 ounces freshly grated cheddar cheese

6 to 8 ounces pulled BBQ pork (see BBQ Pork Butt recipe in Chapter 11)

4 ounces Basic BBQ Sauce (see Chapter 13)

1 cup canned black beans, rinsed and drained

¼ cup diced green bell peppers, ¼-inch dice

½ cup diced tomatoes, ¼-inch dice

¼ cup sliced, pickled jalapeño peppers

1 heaping tablespoon sour cream

DIRECTIONS

1 Preheat the grill or smoker to 250 degrees.

2 In a cast-iron skillet, place a layer of tortilla chips.

3 Spread the cheese evenly over the chips.

4 Put the skillet in the grill or smoker on indirect heat and smoke for 15 minutes or until the cheese is melted.

5 Spread the pulled pork evenly over the melted cheese.

6 Pour the barbecue sauce evenly over the nachos.

7 Add the black beans and diced green bell peppers.

8 Place back in the smoker or grill for 15 minutes.

9 Remove from the heat and add the diced tomatoes.

10 Spread the pickled jalapeños evenly and then add the sour cream on top.

11 Serve piping hot.

PER SERVING: *Calories 539 (From Fat 247); Fat 26g (Saturated 9g); Cholesterol 23mg; Sodium 1,103mg; Carbohydrate 51g (Dietary Fiber 6g); Protein 12g.*

TIP: If you don't have time to make the Basic BBQ Sauce, you can use your favorite commercial barbecue sauce instead.

Grilled Stuffed Tomatoes

PREP TIME: ABOUT 20 MIN	COOK TIME: 1 HR	YIELD: 4 SERVINGS

INGREDIENTS

4 medium to large tomatoes

6 ounces lump crabmeat

½ cup mayonnaise

½ cup Italian breadcrumbs

½ cup grated Parmesan cheese, divided

Coarse ground salt to taste

Coarse ground pepper to taste

1 teaspoon olive oil

DIRECTIONS

1 Preheat the grill to 250 degrees.

2 Core out the tops of the tomatoes, creating a large hole in the top of each tomato but leaving the bottoms intact.

3 In a large bowl, combine the crabmeat, mayonnaise, breadcrumbs, and ¼ cup of the Parmesan cheese.

4 Add the salt and pepper.

5 With a spatula, fill the holes in the tomatoes with the stuffing mixture.

6 Place the stuffed tomatoes in a cast-iron skillet and drizzle the olive oil over the top.

7 Sprinkle the remaining ¼ cup of Parmesan cheese over the tops of the tomatoes.

8 Place in the smoker and smoke for 45 minutes to 1 hour. They're done when the mixture is sizzling slightly and the tomatoes are fork tender.

9 Remove from the smoker and serve hot.

PER SERVING: *Calories 311 (From Fat 146); Fat 16g (Saturated 4g); Cholesterol 57mg; Sodium 815mg; Carbohydrate 25g (Dietary Fiber 3g); Protein 18g.*

Kool-Aid Pickles

PREP TIME: ABOUT 10 MIN PLUS 3–7 DAYS FOR STEEPING	COOK TIME: NONE	YIELD: 12 SERVINGS

INGREDIENTS

One 12-ounce jar kosher dill pickle spears

1 to 2 scoops sweetened Kool-Aid in whatever flavor you prefer

DIRECTIONS

1 Open the pickle jar and pour out about ¼ cup of the pickle juice.

2 Add the Kool-Aid to the pickle jar. Use 2 scoops if you like it sweeter, 1 scoop if you like it less sweet.

3 Put the lid back on the pickle jar and shake thoroughly.

4 Refrigerate and let steep for at least 3 days, preferably a week.

5 Serve cold.

PER SERVING: *Calories 12 (From Fat 0); Fat 0g (Saturated 0g); Cholesterol 0mg; Sodium 220mg; Carbohydrate 3g (Dietary Fiber 0g); Protein 0g.*

TIP: I like using Tropical Punch flavored Kool-Aid in this recipe.

TIP: You can save the ¼ cup of pickle juice for the Pimento Cheese recipe in this chapter if you like.

Cucumber and Onion Salad

PREP TIME: ABOUT 20 MIN PLUS 4 HR FOR REFRIGERATING	COOK TIME: 5 MIN	YIELD: 6 SERVINGS

INGREDIENTS

2 large cucumbers

2 large white onions

2 cups white vinegar

½ cup white sugar

DIRECTIONS

1 Slice the cucumbers and onions into rounds ⅛-inch thick. Place them in a bowl and set aside.

2 In a medium saucepan, place the vinegar and sugar. Heat on medium while stirring constantly until the sugar is thoroughly dissolved, about 5 minutes.

3 Pour the vinegar and sugar mixture over the onions and cucumbers.

4 Cover and refrigerate at least 4 hours, if not overnight.

5 Serve chilled.

PER SERVING: *Calories 129 (From Fat 2); Fat 0g (Saturated 0g); Cholesterol 0mg; Sodium 13mg; Carbohydrate 29g (Dietary Fiber 1g); Protein 2g.*

Cowboy Caviar

PREP TIME: 30 MIN PLUS 1 HR FOR REFRIGERATING	COOK TIME: NONE	YIELD: 6 SERVINGS

INGREDIENTS

8 ounces cooked, drained black beans

8 ounces fresh or canned corn off the cob

1 cup diced green bell peppers

1 cup diced red bell peppers

1 cup diced red onion

Coarse-ground salt to taste

Coarse-ground pepper to taste

1 tablespoon minced cilantro

Juice of 1 lime

DIRECTIONS

1 In a large bowl, place the beans, corn, green and red bell peppers, and onion; mix thoroughly.

2 Add the salt and pepper.

3 Sprinkle on the cilantro.

4 Add the lime juice to the mixture.

5 Mix again.

6 Refrigerate for 1 hour and serve cold.

PER SERVING: *Calories 98 (From Fat 5); Fat 1g (Saturated 0g); Cholesterol 0mg; Sodium 152mg; Carbohydrate 21g (Dietary Fiber 5g); Protein 4g.*

Chapter **15**

Sides

B arbecue sides can make a meal. You can get all kinds of creative with the sides you make on the grill. In this chapter, I show you how a side dish can be a piece of meat's best friend.

TIP

Investing in a barbecue basket and grill screen can help with sides if you want to grill something that could potentially fall through the grate. I talk more about tools in Chapter 3.

As with all barbecue, remember that smoke is an ingredient — you don't want too much of it.

Smoked Green Beans

INGREDIENTS

6 cups green beans, trimmed and chopped into 1-inch pieces

2 cups water

2 tablespoons apple cider vinegar

¼ onion cut into slivers

¼ pound bacon, diced

2 teaspoons pepper, or to taste

1 teaspoon salt, or to taste

DIRECTIONS

1 Preheat the grill or smoker to 250 degrees.

2 In a large casserole dish, place all the ingredients.

3 Place the dish in the smoker, uncovered.

4 Smoke for 3 hours, stirring once an hour.

5 Remove from the smoker and serve hot.

PER SERVING: *Calories 85 (From Fat 46); Fat 5g (Saturated 2g); Cholesterol 12mg; Sodium 482mg; Carbohydrate 5g (Dietary Fiber 2g); Protein 5g.*

BBQ Beans

INGREDIENTS

Two 28-ounce cans plain baked beans

½ cup diced bell peppers, ¼-inch dice

½ cup diced onion, ¼-inch dice

½ cup brown sugar

½ cup Basic BBQ Sauce (see Chapter 13)

2 tablespoons Basic BBQ Rub (Pork Rub) (see Chapter 12)

½ pound bacon, diced

1 cup lard or drippings from cooking a pork butt (see BBQ Pork Butt in Chapter 11)

DIRECTIONS

1 Preheat the grill or smoker to 250 degrees.

2 Add all the ingredients to the cast-iron skillet or large casserole dish.

3 Place the uncovered pan or dish on the smoker on indirect heat.

4 Smoke for 3 hours, stirring once an hour.

5 Remove from the smoker, stir thoroughly, and serve hot.

PER SERVING: *Calories 514 (From Fat 276); Fat 31g (Saturated 11g); Cholesterol 44mg; Sodium 1,244mg; Carbohydrate 48g (Dietary Fiber 7g); Protein 16g.*

TIP: If you're cooking a pork butt, omit the lard and place the skillet or dish under the butt while it cooks, letting the pork grease drip into the beans.

Roasted Corn and Black Bean Salad

PREP TIME: 10 MIN	COOK TIME: 30 MIN	YIELD: 6 SERVINGS

INGREDIENTS

6 ears freshly shucked corn

1 large can black beans, rinsed and drained

1 cup diced red onion, ¼-inch dice

¼ cup minced cilantro

Coarse-ground salt to taste

Coarse-ground black pepper to taste

DIRECTIONS

1 Preheat the grill or smoker to 350 degrees.

2 Place the shucked corn on the grate over direct heat.

3 Grill the corn until it is tender and has a slight char, approximately 20 minutes.

4 Remove the corn from the grill and let cool.

5 When the corn is cool, remove the corn from the cob by setting an ear on its point in a wide or shallow dish and slicing down all around.

6 In a large bowl, place the corn, black beans, onion, and cilantro and mix thoroughly.

7 Add the salt and pepper.

8 Refrigerate for 1 hour and serve cold.

PER SERVING: *Calories 216 (From Fat 18); Fat 2g (Saturated 0g); Cholesterol 0mg; Sodium 299mg; Carbohydrate 46g (Dietary Fiber 10g); Protein 10g.*

VARY IT! To brighten it up, add a squeeze of lemon juice after everything is mixed.

Potato Salad

PREP TIME: 20 MIN	COOK TIME: NONE	YIELD: 6 SERVINGS

INGREDIENTS

1 pound red potatoes boiled, chopped into 1-inch pieces, and cooled

¾ cup mayonnaise

1 cup diced celery

¾ cup diced hot or sweet pickles

1 teaspoon minced fresh or ⅓ teaspoon dried dill

Coarse-ground salt to taste

Coarse-ground black pepper to taste

DIRECTIONS

1 In a large bowl, add the potatoes, mayonnaise, celery, pickles, and dill and mix thoroughly.

2 Salt and pepper to taste.

3 Refrigerate for 1 hour and serve cold.

PER SERVING: *Calories 203 (From Fat 90); Fat 10g (Saturated 1g); Cholesterol 8mg; Sodium 323mg; Carbohydrate 27g (Dietary Fiber 2g); Protein 2g.*

VARY IT! For a mustard potato salad, reduce the amount of mayonnaise to ¼ cup, add ½ cup yellow or Dijon mustard, ¼ cup minced fresh or 1 tablespoon dried chives, 1 teaspoon celery seed, and ½ cup yellow onion. Mix, refrigerate, and enjoy!

Mac and Cheese

PREP TIME: 10 MIN	COOK TIME: 20–40 MIN	YIELD: 6 SERVINGS

INGREDIENTS

¼ cup flour

¼ cup butter

1 cup heavy cream

1 cup diced Velveeta cheese

1 cup diced cream cheese

1 cup shredded cheddar cheese, divided

Coarse-ground salt to taste

1 teaspoon coarse-ground black pepper

2 cups elbow macaroni, cooked and drained

¼ cup Ritz crackers, smashed

DIRECTIONS

1 Preheat the grill or smoker to 350 degrees.

2 In a saucepan on medium heat, mix the flour and butter.

3 Add the heavy cream and stir thoroughly.

4 Add the Velveeta, cream cheese, and ½ cup of the shredded cheddar.

5 Add the salt and add pepper.

6 Stir over medium heat until well mixed.

7 Put the cooked pasta in a cast-iron skillet and pour the cheese mixture over the noodles.

8 Sprinkle the remaining ½ cup of shredded cheddar on top.

9 Sprinkle the crushed Ritz crackers on top.

10 Place in the smoker and cook approximately 15 minutes, until the cheddar on top melts.

11 Remove from the smoker and serve hot.

PER SERVING: *Calories 688 (From Fat 461); Fat 51g (Saturated 31g); Cholesterol 167mg; Sodium 896mg; Carbohydrate 38g (Dietary Fiber 1g); Protein 19g.*

Roasted Street Corn

PREP TIME: 10 MIN | COOK TIME: 30 MIN | YIELD: 6 SERVINGS

INGREDIENTS

½ cup sour cream

½ cup mayonnaise

6 ears freshly shucked corn

1 cup cotija cheese

¼ cup minced cilantro

Ground chipotle powder to taste

DIRECTIONS

1 Preheat the grill or smoker to 350 degrees.

2 In a bowl, mix the sour cream and mayonnaise together. Refrigerate while you prepare the corn.

3 Place the shucked corn on the grill or smoker over direct heat.

4 Grill the corn until it is tender and has a slight char, approximately 20 minutes.

5 Remove the corn from the grill and slather each piece of corn with the mayonnaise–sour cream mixture.

6 Sprinkle the cotija cheese on top.

7 Sprinkle the cilantro and chipotle powder on top.

8 Serve warm.

PER SERVING: *Calories 303 (From Fat 156); Fat 17g (Saturated 7g); Cholesterol 35mg; Sodium 462mg; Carbohydrate 32g (Dietary Fiber 4g); Protein 9g.*

Roasted Grilled Creamed Corn

PREP TIME: 10 MIN	COOK TIME: 30 MIN	YIELD: 6 SERVINGS

INGREDIENTS

6 ears freshly shucked corn

1 tablespoon butter

2 cups heavy cream

¼ cup sugar

1 tablespoon vanilla extract

DIRECTIONS

1 Preheat the grill or smoker to 350 degrees.

2 Place the shucked corn on the grate over direct heat.

3 Grill the corn until it is tender and has a slight char, approximately 20 minutes.

4 Remove the corn from the grill and let cool.

5 Remove the kernels from each ear by cutting them off with a sharp knife; set aside.

6 In a medium saucepan, slowly melt the butter.

7 Place the corn in the pan with the butter.

8 Add the cream, sugar, and vanilla, stirring constantly on medium heat.

9 Stir for 30 minutes, reducing the mixture down to a creamy consistency and sweet flavor.

10 Serve hot.

PER SERVING: *Calories 446 (From Fat 297); Fat 33g (Saturated 20g); Cholesterol 114mg; Sodium 65mg; Carbohydrate 38g (Dietary Fiber 4g); Protein 6g.*

Greens

PREP TIME: 20 MIN	COOK TIME: 2½ HR	YIELD: 6 SERVINGS

INGREDIENTS

2 pounds greens, de-stemmed and chopped (see Note)

½ teaspoon cayenne pepper

½ teaspoon black pepper

1 bay leaf

½ teaspoon ground thyme

¼ teaspoon allspice

4 cups chicken stock

2 tablespoons vegetable shortening

½ pound salted pork or ham, cut into small cubes

½ cup chopped yellow onions

1 garlic clove, minced

DIRECTIONS

1 In a stockpot, add the greens, cayenne pepper, black pepper, bay leaf, thyme, allspice, chicken stock, and enough water to cover the greens; stir thoroughly.

2 Cook the greens on medium heat until tender, approximately 30 minutes.

3 In a separate pan, add the shortening, salted pork or ham, onions, and garlic.

4 Cook on medium heat for about 10 minutes, stirring constantly until the onions are clear.

5 Add the ham to the greens mixture, cover, and simmer everything for 2 hours or until the beans are tender.

6 Serve hot.

PER SERVING: *Calories 157 (From Fat 71); Fat 8g (Saturated 2g); Cholesterol 28mg; Sodium 1,118mg; Carbohydrate 13g (Dietary Fiber 5g); Protein 10g.*

NOTE: You can use turnip, cabbage, mustard, spinach, or any type of greens — or use multiple types!

VARY IT! If you like your greens a little tangy, add ¼ cup apple cider vinegar in Step 5.

TIP: For a real treat, serve the hot greens over mayo-based potato salad for a greens gumbo. (See the Potato Salad recipe earlier in this chapter.)

Grilled Pineapple Salad

PREP TIME: 30 MIN	COOK TIME: 10 MIN	YIELD: 6 SERVINGS

INGREDIENTS

1 pineapple, cored and sliced in 1-inch slices

1 cup diced red onion diced, ¼-inch dice

1 cup diced cucumber, ¼-inch dice

1 tablespoon minced cilantro

1 lime, juiced

Coarse-ground salt to taste

Coarse-ground black pepper to taste

1 avocado, diced

DIRECTIONS

1 Preheat the grill or smoker to 300 degrees.

2 Place the pineapple slices on direct heat.

3 Grill until the slices are slightly charred and the sugars have caramelized on the outside. Keep a very close watch — they can burn very easily.

4 Set aside to cool.

5 When the pineapple has cooled, cut it into ½-inch chunks.

6 In a large bowl, place the pineapple chunks, onions, cucumber, and cilantro, and toss.

7 Add the lime juice, salt, and pepper, and toss again.

8 Fold in the avocado.

9 Refrigerate for 1 hour and serve cold.

PER SERVING: *Calories 142 (From Fat 46); Fat 5g (Saturated 1g); Cholesterol 0mg; Sodium 5mg; Carbohydrate 26g (Dietary Fiber 5g); Protein 2g.*

Grilled Roasted Potatoes

PREP TIME: 10 MIN	COOK TIME: 45 MIN	YIELD: 4 SERVINGS

INGREDIENTS

1 quart quartered mini red potatoes

2 teaspoons olive oil

¼ cup fresh or 1 tablespoon dried rosemary

¼ cup fresh or 1 tablespoon dried thyme

1 teaspoon coarse-ground kosher salt

1 teaspoon coarse-ground pepper

DIRECTIONS

1 Preheat the grill or smoker to 300 degrees.

2 Put a cast-iron skillet in the grill to preheat it.

3 In a bowl, place the potatoes. Drizzle the olive oil on the potatoes, and toss to coat them evenly.

4 Add the rosemary and thyme, and toss.

5 Add the salt and pepper to taste, and toss.

6 Put the potatoes in the preheated iron skillet and roast in the grill for 30 to 45 minutes, until they're fork tender. Check the potatoes frequently and turn them so that they don't burn.

7 Serve hot.

PER SERVING: *Calories 125 (From Fat 22); Fat 2g (Saturated 0g); Cholesterol 0mg; Sodium 289mg; Carbohydrate 24g (Dietary Fiber 3g); Protein 3g.*

Grilled Brussels Sprouts

PREP TIME: 10 MIN	COOK TIME: 45 MIN	YIELD: 6 SERVINGS

INGREDIENTS

1 quart brussels sprouts, halved

2 tablespoons olive oil

Coarse-ground salt to taste

Coarse-ground black pepper to taste

1 cup diced, raw bacon

¼ cup white sugar

½ cup balsamic vinegar

DIRECTIONS

1 Preheat the grill or smoker to 350 degrees.

2 In a medium bowl, toss the brussels sprouts with the olive oil.

3 Add the salt and pepper.

4 Place the brussels sprouts over direct heat and let them cook, turning often, for about 15 minutes or until slightly charred.

5 In a cast-iron skillet, cook the bacon on medium heat until it becomes crispy and the fat melts.

6 Remove the cooked bits and save the grease in the skillet.

7 Add the charred brussels sprouts and the sugar to the skillet with the bacon grease.

8 Toss thoroughly in the skillet and put back over direct heat on the grill.

9 Let cook another 15 minutes while tossing.

10 Add the balsamic vinegar and cook for another 5 minutes.

11 Add the bacon bits and mix everything together.

12 Remove from the grill and serve hot.

PER SERVING: *Calories 290 (From Fat 196); Fat 22g (Saturated 6g); Cholesterol 26mg; Sodium 336mg; Carbohydrate 17g (Dietary Fiber 2g); Protein 6g.*

Black Bean and Corn Salad

PREP TIME: 10 MIN	COOK TIME: 30 MIN	YIELD: 6 SERVINGS

INGREDIENTS

4 ears freshly shucked corn

2 cups black beans, drained and rinsed

1 cup diced red onion, ¼-inch dice

¼ cup minced cilantro

1 tablespoon olive oil

Coarse-ground salt to taste

Coarse-ground black pepper to taste

DIRECTIONS

1 Preheat the grill or smoker to 350 degrees.

2 Place the shucked corn on the grill over direct heat.

3 Grill the corn until it is tender and has a slight char, approximately 20 minutes.

4 Remove the corn from the grill, and let it cool for 10 minutes.

5 Take a knife and, in a downward motion along each side, cut the kernels off the cob.

6 In a bowl, place the corn, black beans, onion, cilantro, and olive oil, and mix thoroughly.

7 Add the salt and pepper.

8 Serve warm or chilled.

PER SERVING: *Calories 185 (From Fat 33); Fat 4g (Saturated 1g); Cholesterol 0mg; Sodium 323mg; Carbohydrate 34g (Dietary Fiber 9g); Protein 8g.*

Coleslaw

INGREDIENTS

1 head green cabbage, shredded

1 cup shredded purple cabbage

1 cup shredded carrot

2 cups Alabama White Sauce (see Chapter 13)

Coarse-ground salt to taste

Coarse-ground black pepper to taste

DIRECTIONS

1 In a bowl, place all the ingredients and mix thoroughly.

2 If needed, add more white sauce for taste and consistency.

3 Add the salt and pepper.

4 Refrigerate for 30 minutes and serve cold.

PER SERVING: *Calories 356 (From Fat 208); Fat 23g (Saturated 3g); Cholesterol 18mg; Sodium 541mg; Carbohydrate 38g (Dietary Fiber 6g); Protein 4g.*

VARY IT! Substitute 2 cups of Vinegar BBQ Sauce (see Chapter 13) for the Alabama White Sauce for a vinegar coleslaw.

VARY IT! Make red coleslaw by using 2 cups of Basic BBQ Sauce (see Chapter 13) instead of the Alabama White Sauce.

Grilled Cauliflower

PREP TIME: 10 MIN | COOK TIME: 20–40 MIN | YIELD: 4 SERVINGS

INGREDIENTS

1 head cauliflower, broken into florets

1 tablespoon olive oil

Large-flake salt to taste

¼ cup shredded Parmesan cheese (optional)

DIRECTIONS

1 Preheat the grill or smoker to 350 degrees.

2 Place a grill basket over direct heat.

3 Place the cauliflower in the basket and drizzle with the olive oil.

4 Sprinkle on the salt.

5 Cook for 20 to 40 minutes, tossing periodically so as not to burn. The cauliflower is done when it's slightly fork tender.

6 If desired, top with grated Parmesan after removing from the grill.

7 Serve hot.

PER SERVING: *Calories 82 (From Fat 32); Fat 4g (Saturated 0g); Cholesterol 0mg; Sodium 63mg; Carbohydrate 11g (Dietary Fiber 5g); Protein 4g.*

Chargrilled Broccolini

PREP TIME: 2 MIN	COOK TIME: 10 MIN	YIELD: 4 SERVINGS

INGREDIENTS

2 bundles broccolini

1 tablespoon olive oil

Large-flake salt to taste

DIRECTIONS

1 Preheat the grill or smoker to 350 degrees.

2 On a sheet tray, lay the broccolini out and drizzle with the olive oil.

3 Sprinkle on the salt.

4 Cook on direct heat, turning constantly, until the broccolini starts to char.

5 Remove from the heat and serve hot.

PER SERVING: *Calories 55 (From Fat 15); Fat 4 g (Saturated 1g); Cholesterol 0mg; Sodium 25mg; Carbohydrate 5g (Dietary Fiber 2g); Protein 2g.*

Chapter **16**

Desserts

Desserts are an integral part of the dining experience, and a barbecue meal is no different. What you enjoy after your meal can be just as memorable as what you eat for your meal.

Some of the desserts in this chapter involve the grill or smoker, and some don't. I hope that these desserts satisfy your sweet tooth and add to your barbecue experience.

Grilled Peaches

PREP TIME: 10 MIN	COOK TIME: 30 MIN	YIELD: 8 SERVINGS

INGREDIENTS

2 tablespoons powdered sugar

1 cup heavy cream

½ tablespoon vanilla

4 fresh ripe peaches, halved and pitted

¼ cup honey

1 lime, juiced

DIRECTIONS

1 Preheat the grill or smoker to 350 degrees.

2 Chill a mixing bowl in the freezer for 10 minutes.

3 In the chilled bowl, add the powdered sugar, cream, and vanilla, and mix, starting on low speed and gradually increasing the speed until the mixture forms peaks.

4 Refrigerate and set aside.

5 Place the peach halves on the grate over direct heat, flat side down.

6 Grill the peaches until they are slightly tender and have a slight char, about 20 minutes.

7 Remove the peaches from the grill and set on a plate, flat side up.

8 Drizzle the peaches with honey and then lime juice.

9 Top with the whipped cream and serve.

PER SERVING: *Calories 177 (From Fat 101); Fat 11g (Saturated 7g); Cholesterol 41mg; Sodium 12mg; Carbohydrate 20g (Dietary Fiber 1g); Protein 1g.*

Honey Lime Watermelon

PREP TIME: 20 MIN   COOK TIME: 50 MIN   YIELD: 12 SERVINGS

INGREDIENTS

1 ripe watermelon

Tajín Clásico seasoning to taste

¼ cup honey

2 whole limes

DIRECTIONS

1 Quarter the watermelon and cut into 1-inch slices.

2 Sprinkle a light covering of Tajín Clásico seasoning on the watermelon.

3 Drizzle with the honey.

4 Squeeze the limes evenly on the watermelon.

5 Chill for 1 hour and serve cold.

PER SERVING: *Calories 126 (From Fat 5); Fat 1g (Saturated 0g); Cholesterol 0mg; Sodium 4mg; Carbohydrate 32g (Dietary Fiber 1g); Protein 2g.*

Apple Pie

PREP TIME: 20 MIN | COOK TIME: 50 MIN | YIELD: 8 SERVINGS

INGREDIENTS

1 quart green apples, cored, peeled, and diced

½ cup sugar

½ cup light brown sugar

3 tablespoons all-purpose flour

1 teaspoon cinnamon

1 tablespoon lemon juice

2 frozen premade piecrusts

DIRECTIONS

1 Preheat the oven to 375 degrees.

2 In a mixing bowl, add the apples, sugar, brown sugar, flour, cinnamon, and lemon juice, and stir lightly.

3 Pour the contents into 1 piecrust.

4 Use the second piecrust to cover the mix. Cut out a design if you like.

5 Place in the oven on the lower rack and bake for 50 minutes.

6 Let cool slightly and serve hot.

PER SERVING: *Calories 307 (From Fat 102); Fat 11g (Saturated 4g); Cholesterol 0mg; Sodium 180mg; Carbohydrate 49g (Dietary Fiber 2g); Protein 3g.*

Fudge Pie

PREP TIME: 10 MIN   COOK TIME: 50 MIN   YIELD: 8 SERVINGS

INGREDIENTS

⅓ cup butter

⅔ cup sugar

½ cup cocoa powder

3 eggs

1 cup light corn syrup

¼ teaspoon salt

1 frozen premade piecrust

DIRECTIONS

1 Preheat the oven to 375 degrees.

2 In a saucepan, melt the butter over low heat.

3 Add the sugar and cocoa, and stir until the sugar is melted into the mixture; set aside while you whip the eggs.

4 In a separate bowl, whip the eggs; add the corn syrup and salt.

5 Add the egg mixture to the butter and cocoa mixture, and stir thoroughly.

6 Pour the contents into the piecrust.

7 Place in the oven on the lower rack and cook for 50 minutes.

8 Let cool slightly and serve hot.

PER SERVING: *Calories 390 (From Fat 143); Fat 16g (Saturated 8g); Cholesterol 99mg; Sodium 269mg; Carbohydrate 63g (Dietary Fiber 2g); Protein 5g.*

CHAPTER 16 **Desserts**   211

Grilled Peach Cobbler

PREP TIME: 20 MIN	COOK TIME: 1 HR	YIELD: 8 SERVINGS

INGREDIENTS

1 quart peaches, peeled, pitted, and diced

½ cup sugar

½ cup light brown sugar

3 tablespoons cornstarch

1 teaspoon cinnamon

1 tablespoon lemon juice

2 frozen premade piecrusts

DIRECTIONS

1 Preheat the grill or smoker to 350 degrees.

2 In a mixing bowl, add the peaches, sugar, brown sugar, cornstarch, cinnamon, and lemon juice. Stir lightly to mix.

3 Grease a medium (8- to 10-inch) cast-iron skillet and line with a piecrust thawed enough to be pliable.

4 Pour the peach mixture into the piecrust.

5 Use the second piecrust to cover. Cut out a design if you like.

6 Place on the smoker over indirect heat.

7 Cook in the smoker for 1 hour.

8 Remove from the smoker, let cool slightly, and serve hot.

PER SERVING: *Calories 320 (From Fat 103); Fat 11g (Saturated 4g); Cholesterol 0mg; Sodium 180mg; Carbohydrate 52g (Dietary Fiber 2g); Protein 3g.*

Chocolate Pie

PREP TIME: 20 MIN | COOK TIME: 40 MIN | YIELD: 12 SERVINGS

INGREDIENTS

4 ounces semisweet baking chocolate

½ cup melted unsalted butter

1 cup granulated sugar

1½ teaspoons vanilla

2 eggs

1 piecrust, frozen or fresh

DIRECTIONS

1 Preheat the oven to 350 degrees.

2 In a saucepan, melt the chocolate over low heat.

3 Add the butter and sugar, stirring until the mixture is smooth.

4 Stir in the vanilla and remove from the stove, cooling for 3 to 5 minutes.

5 In a separate bowl, whisk the eggs until thoroughly mixed.

6 Add the eggs to the chocolate mixture, blending thoroughly.

7 Pour into a piecrust.

8 Cook for 30 minutes on the lower rack; then move the pie to the top rack and cook for another 10 minutes.

9 Remove from the oven, cool on the countertop for 30 minutes, and serve.

PER SERVING: *Calories 257 (From Fat 155); Fat 17g (Saturated 9g); Cholesterol 56mg; Sodium 74mg; Carbohydrate 27g (Dietary Fiber 2g); Protein 3g.*

TIP: Top with whipped cream or ice cream before serving, if you like.

Grilled Bananas Foster

PREP TIME: 20 MIN	COOK TIME: 10 MIN	YIELD: 4 SERVINGS

INGREDIENTS

2 whole bananas sliced lengthwise and cut in half

4 tablespoons butter

½ cup brown sugar

½ cup Peg Leg Porker Bourbon or bourbon or rum of your choice

1 pint vanilla bean ice cream

DIRECTIONS

1 Preheat the grill or smoker to 250 degrees.

2 Put the bananas on the grill, flat side down, over direct heat.

3 Grill for 2 to 5 minutes and get a little char on them.

4 Remove from the grill and set aside.

5 In a steel or cast-iron skillet, place the butter and brown sugar.

6 Place on the grill, stirring constantly, until the butter and sugar are melted together.

7 Add the bourbon, and using a long stick lighter, light the dish on fire. *Note:* Be very careful about your surroundings and the grill or smoker hood. The flames can extend about 18 to 20 inches, so make sure that you have a clear area to flambé.

8 Let the skillet flame up, constantly stirring.

9 Put the bananas into the skillet and cook for approximately 3 minutes, until the flame goes out.

10 Divide the ice cream between 4 bowls.

11 Ladle the bananas over the ice cream and enjoy.

PER SERVING: *Calories 554 (From Fat 261); Fat 29g (Saturated 18g); Cholesterol 129mg; Sodium 153mg; Carbohydrate 55g (Dietary Fiber 2g); Protein 5g.*

Apple Crisp

PREP TIME: 20 MIN | COOK TIME: 45–60 MIN | YIELD: 6 SERVINGS

INGREDIENTS

1 green apple, peeled, cored, and diced

1 teaspoon cinnamon

1 teaspoon lemon juice

2 tablespoons sugar

1 cup whole grain oats

1 cup brown sugar

½ cup butter, diced

¾ cup flour

DIRECTIONS

1 Preheat the grill or smoker to 350 degrees.

2 In a bowl combine the apple, cinnamon, lemon juice, and sugar; mix thoroughly.

3 Transfer the mixture to a cast-iron skillet and set on the grill over indirect heat.

4 In a separate bowl, mix the oats, brown sugar, butter, and flour together, blending well.

5 Spread the oat mixture on top of the apple mixture in the skillet.

6 Bake in the grill or smoker for 45 minutes to 1 hour, until bubbly.

7 Let cool a bit and serve.

PER SERVING: *Calories 365 (From Fat 148); Fat 16g (Saturated 10g); Cholesterol 41mg; Sodium 117mg; Carbohydrate 52g (Dietary Fiber 2g); Protein 4g.*

Smoked Whipped Cream

PREP TIME: 10 MIN   COOK TIME: 20 MIN   YIELD: 8 SERVINGS

INGREDIENTS

1 cup cold whipping cream

2 quarts ice cubes

2 tablespoons powdered sugar

½ teaspoon vanilla

DIRECTIONS

1 Preheat the grill or smoker to 200 degrees.

2 In a nonreactive dish, place the whipping cream.

3 Place that dish in a stainless-steel bowl, and surround the dish with ice.

4 Place the bowl on the smoker over indirect heat.

5 Lightly smoke for 20 minutes; then remove from the smoker.

6 Add the powdered sugar and vanilla.

7 Pour any remaining ice or water out of the stainless-steel bowl and pour the cream into it.

8 Whip until the cream forms peaks.

9 Chill for at least 1 hour before serving.

PER SERVING: *Calories 110 (From Fat 99); Fat 11g (Saturated 7g); Cholesterol 41mg; Sodium 11mg; Carbohydrate 3g (Dietary Fiber 0g); Protein 1g.*

Blueberry Pie

PREP TIME: 10 MIN | COOK TIME: 50 MIN | YIELD: 8 SERVINGS

INGREDIENTS

1 pint blueberries, washed

¾ cup sugar

3 tablespoons cornstarch

½ teaspoon cinnamon

1 teaspoon lemon zest

2 frozen premade piecrusts

DIRECTIONS

1 Preheat the grill or smoker to 375 degrees.

2 In a bowl, place the blueberries, sugar, cornstarch, cinnamon, and lemon zest; stir lightly to mix.

3 Pour into 1 piecrust.

4 Use the second piecrust to cover. Cut out a design if you like.

5 Place the pie in the oven on the lower rack for 50 minutes.

6 Let cool for 10 minutes and serve hot.

PER SERVING: *Calories 301 (From Fat 103); Fat 11g (Saturated 4g); Cholesterol 0mg; Sodium 178mg; Carbohydrate 48g (Dietary Fiber 2g); Protein 3g.*

5

The Part of Tens

IN THIS CHAPTER

» Paying attention to the cooking

» Getting the tools and the attire right

» Getting everything ready and then relaxing

Chapter **17**

Ten Rookie Mistakes to Avoid

C ooking barbecue is fun, but nothing can ruin your fun faster than messing up your Q. Because it takes so long to cook, you need to make sure you get it right. There's no time for do-overs when you're on a schedule with people coming over. Here are ten rookie mistakes to avoid.

Not Paying Close Attention to Temperature

Barbecue is all about time and temperature. You want a consistency to your cook. In other words, you want to keep your temperature even and not have it spike up or down. If you're cooking at 250 degrees, you want to stay at 250 degrees. That's not always the easiest thing to do, so what you really aim for is not going over 260 degrees or below 240 degrees. Wide temperature variations can mess up your barbecue.

Many beginners get their fire too hot — a mistake you want to avoid. When you cook too fast, especially with barbecue cuts, the muscle contracts and the collagen becomes tough instead of breaking down and becoming tender.

TIP

If your fire's too hot, take the time to let it cool down and make sure that when your meat goes on, it's going on at the right temperature. (Turn to Chapter 2 for temperature info.)

The skill to regulate temperature and avoid spikes comes as you get familiar with the ins and outs of your grill.

Not Being Prepared

I can't tell you how many times I've started to cook only to realize that I didn't have everything I needed to complete the cook. Do yourself a favor and make a list. Write down everything you know you're going to need and everything you think you may need.

Make sure you have enough fuel. Make sure you have the right tools — tongs, gloves, grill brushes, basting liquid, spray bottle, and anything else you can think you may need while you're cooking.

Because you're cooking barbecue, you may have time to go to the store in the middle of your cook, but you certainly don't want to *have* to. Often when you're cooking barbecue, you may be having a drink, and I certainly don't recommend leaving your house if that's the case.

Over-Smoking Your Meat

Some wood smoke (such as hickory) is very powerful, and some cuts of meat (such as ribs) are fairly thin. You can easily over-smoke ribs and other small cuts of meat. If you've ever done it, you know it's not something you want to repeat.

Try to match your wood with the cut of meat and your desired flavor profile, and smoke with just enough to impart the right amount of flavor to your meat. (Turn to Chapter 2 for tips on pairing meat with wood.) Remember that your meat only takes on smoke up to about 125 degrees — after that you're just piling pollutants onto the meat.

If you're cooking a large cut of meat, it's fairly hard to over-smoke. Some cuts, such as brisket or whole hog, prefer a lot of smoke.

TIP

What you're looking for is a clear blue smoke, not a white billowy one. If your cooker is billowing a big plume of white smoke, your meat is probably absorbing a bitter, acrid flavor — something you want to avoid. Open the cooker properly and let the smoke burn off.

WARNING

Be careful when opening a grill with lots of smoke coming out. Opening the smoker lid all at once can create a fireball, which is not something you want in your face. Puff the lid by lifting it an inch and then closing it again to dissipate some of the smoke. Do this two or three times before fully opening the lid.

Using Too Much Seasoning

When it comes to seasoning your meat, don't overdo it. Remember that sometimes less is more. Start out with an even amount of rub that coats the surface but doesn't cake it. See how that turns out. A good rub accentuates the flavor of the meat and doesn't overpower it. Moderation is key. Your guests want to eat your ribs not just your rub.

REMEMBER

Part of the fun of barbecue is doing it over and over again, not only to find out what you like but also to perfect your technique.

Not Wearing the Proper Clothes

Don't wear your Sunday best when you're cooking barbecue. Barbecue is messy, and so are grills. Trust me, if you're doing it right, you're going to get dirty. You may end up with grease stains or a hole in your shirt, so wear clothes that can stand up to barbecue. Having a good apron handy helps, too.

WARNING

Don't cook barbecue in flip-flops. Coals are hot, and they drop out of the bottom of smokers or out of the bottom of grills all the time. You don't want an exposed foot when a hot coal drops out of your smoker. You can thank me later.

Not Using the Proper Wood

Cooking barbecue involves using wood. Make sure you understand what you have on hand and how it flavors your meat. (Chapter 2 goes into detail about fuel and flavors.)

Make sure you have the right size wood. If you have a small grill or small smoker, you want chips or chunks. If you have a large smoker, you probably want logs, but make sure they're cut to a manageable size. When using a stick burner, make sure you have pieces that are smaller or split more thoroughly so that you can control the heat like you're using a fine-tuned oven. Larger chunks are hard to control and can often burn too hot. Flexibility is key here. Larger chunks of wood equal a larger heat source; smaller chunks of wood equal a more fine-tuned heat source.

You also need to factor in the age or dryness of your wood. If you're using very dry wood, it'll burn faster and hotter. Greener wood burns slower but also puts off more smoke. Many people using horizontal offset smokers use a combination of dry and green wood to achieve their desired effect.

Trusting a Bad Thermometer or Placing Your Thermometer in a Bad Spot

When cooking barbecue, a reliable and accurate thermometer is key. Many backyard grills and smokers come with very cheap thermometers. You may want to invest in a digital thermometer to replace the one that came with your smoker. (I talk about essential barbecue tools in Chapter 3.)

Thermometer placement is also key. You need to know what the temperature is inside your smoker, but more important, what the temperature is where your meat is sitting at grate level. If you place your thermometer too high on the door of the smoker, you can get a bad reading and waste a lot of time. If you find this to be the case, you may want to drill a hole in the door of your smoker and place a temperature probe or thermometer at grate level. You want the thermometer as close to the level of your meat as possible.

Equally important as the temperature inside your smoker is the temperature inside your meat. Many great digital probes measure the internal temperature of meat as you cook. Many digital probes have multiple thermocouples (sensors), too.

TIP

If you're using a multi-probe thermometer, you can place one probe beside the meat on the actual grate inside the smoker and one probe directly into the muscle of the meat. That way you can track not only the internal temperature of the smoker but also the progress of your meat as it cooks.

Powering through the Stall

If you're cooking a large piece of meat — a brisket, a pork shoulder, a Boston butt, or even a whole hog — your meat will stall at 160 degrees. What does that mean? Well, as the meat cooks, you see the internal temperature steadily rise and rise until it hits 160 degrees. The temperature then stops rising and remains at 160 degrees. This stall is common and is a result of the chemistry of the cell structure in the meat reacting to heat. Don't fear the stall — it happens. It's part of the cook.

The rookie mistake is to panic and crank up the temperature of the smoker to try to make it through the stall. Don't do that. When your meat hits the stall point, sit back, relax, and enjoy a nice drink while you wait. Keep your temperature the same as it has been the whole cook. The meat will make it through the stall with no adjustment.

The stall may last 30 minutes, or it may last three hours. Eventually, the temperature of the meat will rise again, and when it does, you're not too far from your target temperature of 192 degrees. So, power through the stall with focus, patience, and an understanding that this, too, shall pass. Patience is the key to success.

Being Too Rushed

Barbecue takes time. To be a successful barbecue cook, you need to be patient. Consult one of the many charts out there for reference on how long a cook should take based on the temperature that you want to cook, and give yourself the proper amount of time. (You can find a good reference at www.smokedbbqsource.com/smoking-times-temperatures.) Actually, give yourself more time than you think you'll need.

REMEMBER

Your meat needs time to cook at the right temperature, and it also needs time to rest after your cook is complete, so make sure to allow for both these times when planning your cook.

People who don't plan ahead often need to rush their cooks in order for them to be ready for an event or a party. When that happens they typically crank up the heat and end up ruining what would have otherwise been a deliciously cooked barbecue meal.

REMEMBER

I can't say often enough that barbecue is not rocket science, but it does require the proper time and temperature. If either one of those elements is off, you run the risk of ruining your good Q. You want to smoke your meat between 190 and 250 degrees, depending on what you're cooking, and you need to allow enough time for the meat to reach an internal temperature of 192 degrees for larger cuts.

Stressing Out

It's easy to stress out about barbecue. If you haven't cooked a lot, the pressure can get to you. Because cooking barbecue takes a good deal of time, it's easy to get stressed when it doesn't turn out right. It's not like you can just turn around and make another burger patty and have it be done in ten minutes. When you mess up barbecue, you're in for a long night. The best way to avoid this scenario is by avoiding the nine rookie mistakes in the previous sections.

Barbecue should be about having fun with your family and friends. You're not curing cancer here — you're just trying to make sure that people have a good time and a great meal. If you approach your barbecue with that attitude, and if you take the time to get it right, barbecue can turn out to be a lifelong obsession.

TIP

When you cook barbecue, have a buddy over or a family member or your children. It's about friends and family and enjoying the time you have together. The process of cooking barbecue is a long one, and that allows for time to visit with family and friends, reflect on the day, enjoy the outdoors, and learn something new. Stressing out doesn't help at all. Practice makes perfect, and what better way to have fun than by cooking barbecue often to perfect your craft?

Chapter **18**

Ten Questions to Ask Your Butcher

Having a great relationship with your butcher can be wonderful for your barbecue. If you have a neighborhood butcher you like, I suggest building a great rapport with her by visiting often. In this chapter, I give you ten questions to ask your butcher.

Where Do You Source Your Meat?

Understanding where your meat comes from is always important. What you want is quality. You're looking for meat that's ethically raised and doesn't contain added hormones or additives such as phosphates. A good meat source has a U.S. Department of Agriculture (USDA) inspection label. Information on the label enables you to look up the source and read about its farming practices.

Look for a source with a consistent track record. For example, certain industry groups have come together to make sure that all their producers follow strict guidelines. One such group is Certified Angus Beef, which provides its stamp of approval only to beef providers that follow specific practices. Look to see whether your source is a member of an industry group that demands standards that go above and beyond government rules and guidelines.

Some butchers source locally and have meat from nearby local or family farms; others don't. If local is important to you, you can probably find a butcher close by to provide you with meat from a local farm. But keep in mind that just because it's local, doesn't mean it's any better.

What Interesting Cuts Do You Have Available?

A great question to ask your butcher is what interesting cuts he has available. Butchers have access to some lesser-known cuts that you may not see in your grocery store.

One such cut is a hanger steak or what some call *butcher's tenderloin*. I was first introduced to this cut by my butcher, and I absolutely love it. The texture is meaty, and it's bloodier than many other cuts, giving it a very robust and flavorful taste.

TIP

Ask your butcher about these unique cuts. He may have something you've never heard of that turns out to be your new favorite cut of meat. Meat trends evolve and creative butchers are always looking for new cuts to offer.

How Do I Prepare a Particular Cut of Meat?

Your butcher can help you find a new cut of meat. She also should be able to tell you how to prepare that cut of meat. A butcher should be able to tell you how to prepare any cut of meat she sells you.

A great butcher shop has recipes that you can follow for particular cuts of meat they sell. If the recipes aren't right out in the open, ask your butcher if she has suggestions.

Can You Make Me a Custom Cut?

Don't be afraid to ask your butcher for a custom cut. If you like your rib-eye steaks 3 inches thick, your butcher should be able to make it so. A good butcher won't question why you want a 3-inch piece of rib-eye; he'll just cut it for you.

If your butcher isn't willing to cut custom steaks for you, find a new butcher. As long as you're willing to pay for a particular cut and it's not wasteful for the butcher, he should be able to accommodate your request.

I remember a particular grocery store I used to go to because they had great sales on rib-eyes and New York strips. I would ask the butcher to cut me eight to ten of a particular cut at a certain thickness. That butcher always seemed annoyed at my special request; I was the one who was *really* annoyed.

A butcher's job is to cut meat. A good butcher takes pride in making cuts how you prefer a certain way.

The cut you're asking for shouldn't leave waste for the butcher to deal with. If your special cut leaves waste that the butcher can't sell, you should be prepared to purchase those extra trimmings.

How Do I Slice This Piece of Meat to Make It the Most Useful and Tender?

How you slice a piece of meat affects the experience of eating it.

Some meats are the most flavorful when cut along the grain, and that's the texture you expect from that particular cut of meat. However, some cuts of meat need to be cut *across* the grain to be at their most flavorful and tender. Be sure and ask your butcher exactly how to slice the meat after it's prepared in order to give the best experience to you and your guests.

Brisket is a good example of a cut that needs to be sliced a certain way to ensure the best end result. When cutting brisket, you start with the flat and cut across the grain. When you get to the point, or the upper muscle of the brisket, you turn it 90 degrees and cut it from that side so that the meat on the point is cut across the grain and not with the grain.

Do You Have Serving Suggestions for Me?

A butcher you visit frequently is generally happy to give you dinner suggestions or point out particular cuts of meat you may like. A good butcher pays attention to the types of meat you buy and listens to your feedback about the meat you bought last time. Like a good bartender, that butcher can then suggest a new cut of meat you may find appealing and meals that you may want to prepare with that particular cut of meat.

REMEMBER

Listen to your butcher. She can be a great educator. She loves great food just like you do, and she's in the meat business for a reason. A great butcher has a passion for what she does and, obviously, a love of meat. Welcome the opportunity to let your butcher suggest a cut of meat or give a dinner idea based on her knowledge of the meat and your tastes.

How Long Will This Meat Stay Fresh?

Butchers understand their product, and that product is meat. A butcher knows how meat ages, how the meat should be stored and at what temperature, and, most important, how long that particular cut of meat has been in the butcher's case.

TIP

Don't be afraid to ask your butcher the shelf life of the cut of meat you're buying. Some things keep a lot longer than others. Your butcher can tell you that a cut will be good kept in the fridge the way that it's packaged for two days, five days, eight days, or whatever the case may be. You don't want to keep something in your fridge too long and have it spoil.

Do You Have Any Aged Meats?

If you like a great steak, ask your butcher if he has any aged meats. Aging meat helps break down the connective tissue to make it tender and bring out a rich flavor. However, meats need to be aged the proper way. Some meats are *wet aged* (aged in the bag that they came in), and some meats are *dry aged* (aged in the open in a controlled temperature and environmentally clean room).

REMEMBER

Wet-aging can be great for steaks — they're more tender than meat that hasn't been aged. However, a dry-aged steak has a more robust flavor and different texture than a steak aged in a bag.

Because a dry-aged steak loses so much weight, it tends to be much more expensive. Your butcher can guide you in the right direction on what meets your needs and your budget.

Do You Have Any Pre-Prepared Entrees?

Good butcher shops often have some prepared foods. They may have chicken breasts stuffed with Swiss cheese and ham, or custom sausages, or pre-marinated steaks, or a stuffed rack of lamb.

REMEMBER

If an entree is pre-prepared, that doesn't mean that the meat is already cooked and ready to eat. It *does* mean that it's easy for you to pick up, take home, and cook immediately.

Even if you don't see anything in the case, you can ask your butcher about pre-prepared entrees. Butchers often like to get creative, so your butcher may have some great items that he knows work well together and have them already prepared. Likewise, if you see something in the case that you don't recognize, ask your butcher about it — she'll be happy to tell you what she has come up with.

What's Your Recommended Burger Blend?

The butchering process produces a lot of trim from all the different cuts too small to be sold alone. These leftovers can go into sausage and can also become part of a burger blend.

A butcher knows exactly what goes together to make a great blend of meats. He can put together a burger blend that is second to none.

Ask your butcher what he feels is the best burger blend and if he has any on hand. He'll not only be happy to tell you but be very proud of what he has put together from the particular cuts of meat that he has used for the week. This is a sense of pride for the butcher and something he'll love to pass on to you.

Chapter **19**

Ten Seasonings to Keep on Hand

Your seasoning drawer is your toolbox for barbecue. In Chapter 12, I talk about how to put ingredients together to make delicious combinations for rubs. In this chapter, I tell you about the essential building blocks for those blends.

Salt

You knew I was gonna say it: Salt is the be-all and end-all for your kitchen. Salt is the ultimate flavor enhancer, and when used correctly, it can take an ordinary cut of meat and turn it into something very flavorful. Salt enhances flavor at its most basic nature.

I keep several types of salt on hand:

» **Table salt:** You need to have some type of salt on hand for your guests if they want to add some flavor to their dish, so make sure that you always have some regular table salt on your dinner table. Table salt is also an ingredient in many recipes. Just look for plain old iodized salt in the grocery aisle.

>> **Kosher salt (medium-flake salt):** Because of the nature of the flakes, you can control how much salt you use in any particular dish with this type of salt. You can find kosher salt in a blue box in the baking aisle. Kosher salt may be labeled *large-flake kosher salt* or just *kosher salt,* depending on the brand. Not all kosher salt has larger flakes. For a medium flake, you want them between $\frac{1}{10}$-inch to $\frac{1}{20}$-inch wide.

>> **Large-flake salt:** This type of salt comes in many forms, including Maldon salt and large-flake sea salt, to name two. Large-flake salt is typically a finishing salt you sprinkle on a finished dish. Because of the large flakes (typically ¼ inch to ½ inch in width), you can control the amount on your finished food more easily.

Pepper

Another basic ingredient, pepper is a familiar spice to most people. It adds a spiciness without being hot. Pepper is quintessential to cooking. Always have pepper around in a few different forms:

>> **Fine-grind pepper:** This is your regular, table-variety pepper. You can buy it in the grocery store in a can and use it in many of your favorite recipes. Make sure you have it on your table for guests to add a spicy finish to an entree if they like.

>> **Coarse-grind pepper:** This is the pepper you're likely to choose for barbecue. Coarse-grind salt and coarse-grind pepper are staples for brisket and beef ribs. The larger nature of coarse-grind pepper allows you to control it more easily than its finer-grind counterpart.

>> **Fresh-cracked pepper:** Have a pepper grinder on hand to make fresh cracked pepper from peppercorns. Fresh cracked pepper is always better than already ground pepper. Just like any spice, it's at the peak of freshness the moment you start to grind it. However, fresh-cracked pepper isn't practical for large applications, such as cooking multiple large cuts of meat.

Garlic Powder

Garlic in powder form is a great spice and is very flavorful. In the barbecue world, it's a key ingredient in many rubs. It's also important in blended sausages, such as kielbasa.

REMEMBER

Garlic powder is different from fresh garlic and imparts a different taste. Many times, the taste of this dehydrated spice makes or breaks a particular barbecue dish.

Onion Powder

You may think that onion powder is very close in nature to garlic powder, but onion powder is actually very different and has a distinctly different taste. The two spices are used together quite often, but they don't have the same effect on the tongue.

WARNING

Be very careful with onion powder. Too much and you definitely know it! Onion powder can overpower a rub when you use too much — and that's not good. Check the rubs recipes in Chapter 12 for tips on proportions.

Cayenne Pepper

Cayenne pepper, sometimes labeled *ground red pepper,* is the most basic way to add heat to a dish or a rub. It's not too spicy, and you can easily manipulate heat with it. Cayenne has a familiar taste because it's used in so many dishes, so you very rarely have to worry about this spice turning someone off.

If you want a little heat without detracting from the flavor, add some cayenne. Unlike other much hotter spices, cayenne tends to complement, and not distract from, the flavor of a dish.

Chili Powder

Chili powder is actually a spice blend that's used like a single spice in many recipes and rubs. Chili powder has a base of cumin, and you definitely taste that in the underlying tones, but it's more complex than a single spice and it can add a layer of depth to your dish or rub.

For barbecue, chili powder is key. The taste is familiar because it's used so often in rubs and seasoning blends, most often with pork or chicken — not so much with beef.

Rosemary

Rosemary is a great seasoning for most meat. It has a strong flavor, but sometimes you need that for larger cuts. Pair it with thyme for a powerful combo.

You can grow rosemary easily and find it just as easily in most grocery stores, either fresh or dried.

You don't see rosemary often in rub recipes except in powdered form. Many barbecue people don't get the fact that it has some great underlying tones that truly complement all meats.

Thyme

I call thyme the sister spice to rosemary. The two are a powerful combination. Thyme is an excellent complement to meat, but it can be used for so many more things — for example, to season drinks, cheeses, tomatoes, and eggs.

Allspice

I like allspice because of its warm overtones of nutmeg, cinnamon, and pepper. It's actually the berry of the Jamaican pepper tree. Allspice can make a great addition to a barbecue rub or seasoning, and it adds some depth and complexity. Not everyone knows how to use allspice properly, but when you get the hang of it, it's a great addition to your spice arsenal. Use it if you want just a touch of sweetness in your rub or seasoning. Start with a very small amount, and then work your way up to taste.

Allspice adds a little hint of sweetness to a rub and brightens it up a bit. It's often used in seasoning blends like jerk seasoning, which originated in Jamaica. I like it in a barbecue seasoning that goes on your meat after it cooks.

Paprika

Paprika is the base of most pork barbecue rubs. Paprika doesn't add a whole lot of flavor, but it provides a base to carry your other flavors and has great color. It comes in many forms, including Hungarian and Spanish. Some people like it plain; others, smoked. I prefer plain Spanish paprika.

Nearly every barbecue chef has paprika on hand. It is, simply put, the multitool of barbecue.

Chapter **20**

Ten Iconic Barbecue Restaurants

The number of great barbecue restaurants all around the country makes it very hard to name the best or the most iconic. All lists, even this one, should be taken with a grain of salt. Most people love what they're familiar with or grew up eating, and I'm no exception.

This chapter highlights notable places that have proved that they're worthy of greatness over a long period of time.

The Rendezvous (Memphis, Tennessee)

One of my favorites of all time, the Rendezvous, established in 1948, is known for inventing a unique style of ribs now known as the dry rib. They don't call it that, though — they just call it the Rendezvous Rib. This unique rib is distinct in the fact that the dry seasoning is put on the rib after it's cooked. For more information, go to www.hogsfly.com or call 901-523-2746.

Arthur Bryant's (Kansas City, Missouri)

Arthur Bryant took the helm of this legendary spot in 1946, having learned from the legendary Henry Perry, who migrated north from Memphis. Bryant went on to make his restaurant one of the most famous barbecue places in the world. For more information, go to www.arthurbryantsbbq.com or call 816-231-1123.

The Bar-B-Q Shop (Memphis, Tennessee)

The Bar-B-Q Shop is a great spot for traditional Memphis barbecue. Known for great ribs and the invention of Bar-B-Q Spaghetti, the Bar-B-Q Shop has a rich history rooted in a building where the current owner's parents lived. For more information, go to http://thebar-b-qshop.com or call 901-272-1277.

Louis Mueller Barbecue (Taylor, Texas)

Known as the king of the Beef Rib, this iconic Texas location has been around since 1949. It has been through some tumultuous family quarrels but still remains one of the top places for Texas barbecue. Now run by Wayne Mueller, you can still get the legendary beef ribs that made them famous. For more information, go to www.louiemuellerbarbecue.com or call 512-352-6206.

Kreuz Market (Lockhart, Texas)

This Texas institution was established in 1875. It has spanned a few different families and many different owners but remains a stalwart in the Texas barbecue community. From its original incarnation to what it is today, this is a don't-miss destination for Texas barbecue. For more information, go to www.kreuzmarket.com or call 512-398-2361.

Skylight Inn BBQ (Ayden, North Carolina)

Pete Jones was just 17 when he opened the Skylight Inn in 1947, and his whole-hog barbecue has been winning awards and rave reviews ever since. Pete's grandson Sam now runs the business and remains committed to his grandfather's standard of wood-only fires. For more information, go to www.skylightinnbbq.com or call 252-746-4113.

Big Bob Gibson Bar-B-Q (Decatur, Alabama)

Big Bob was famous for his white sauce (find my version in Chapter 13), and he made barbecue poultry the standard in his corner of Alabama and beyond. Big Bob may be gone, but his barbecue empire remains firmly in his family's hands. Multiple generations of Gibsons have carried on the family's award-winning barbecue and are approaching 100 years of great barbecue. For more information, go to http://bigbobgibson.com or call 256-350-6969 or 256-350-0404.

17th Street BBQ (Murphysboro, Illinois)

Already a barbecue legend due to the quality of his barbecue empire in southern Illinois, Mike Mills was inducted into the Barbecue Hall of Fame in 2010. (The other Mike Mills was inducted into the Rock & Roll Hall of Fame with the rest of R.E.M. in 2007.) For more information, go to https://17bbq.com or call 618-684-3722.

Lem's Bar-B-Q (Chicago, Illinois)

You may not think Illinois when you think of barbecue meccas, but with 17th Street BBQ in southern Illinois and Lem's Bar-B-Q in Chicago, this Midwest state has tons of barbecue cred. The Lem of Lem's is actually Lemons: Brothers Bruce and Myles Lemons opened their first restaurant in 1954 and have been satisfying barbecue lovers ever since. Lem's is known for rib tips and hot links — a spicy sausage, for those not from the South. For more information, go to http://lemsque.com or call 773-994-2428.

Peg Leg Porker (Nashville, Tennessee)

I would be remiss if I didn't mention my own Peg Leg Porker. Located in Nashville, Tennessee, this restaurant is my life's dream and embodies my experience of barbecue growing up in West Tennessee with influences from the Rendezvous, the Public Eye, John Will's BBQ, and Lewis's Store. At Peg Leg Porker, you find real Tennessee barbecue — it's pork and chicken here. If you want brisket, go to Texas; Peg Leg doesn't serve it. Our most famous item is our smoked, not char-broiled, Dry Ribs, our take on the famous West Tennessee dish. For more information, go to www.peglegporker.com or call 615-829-6023.

6 Appendixes

Appendix A

Metric Conversion Guide

N*ote:* The recipes in this book weren't developed or tested using metric measurements. There may be some variation in quality when converting to metric units.

Common Abbreviations

Abbreviation(s)	What It Stands For
cm	Centimeter
C., c.	Cup
G, g	Gram
kg	Kilogram
L, l	Liter
lb.	Pound
mL, ml	Milliliter
oz.	Ounce
pt.	Pint
t., tsp.	Teaspoon
T., Tb., Tbsp.	Tablespoon

Volume

U.S. Units	Canadian Metric	Australian Metric
¼ teaspoon	1 milliliter	1 milliliter
½ teaspoon	2 milliliters	2 milliliters
1 teaspoon	5 milliliters	5 milliliters
1 tablespoon	15 milliliters	20 milliliters
¼ cup	50 milliliters	60 milliliters
⅓ cup	75 milliliters	80 milliliters
½ cup	125 milliliters	125 milliliters
⅔ cup	150 milliliters	170 milliliters
¾ cup	175 milliliters	190 milliliters
1 cup	250 milliliters	250 milliliters
1 quart	1 liter	1 liter
1½ quarts	1.5 liters	1.5 liters
2 quarts	2 liters	2 liters
2½ quarts	2.5 liters	2.5 liters
3 quarts	3 liters	3 liters
4 quarts (1 gallon)	4 liters	4 liters

Weight

U.S. Units	Canadian Metric	Australian Metric
1 ounce	30 grams	30 grams
2 ounces	55 grams	60 grams
3 ounces	85 grams	90 grams
4 ounces (¼ pound)	115 grams	125 grams
8 ounces (½ pound)	225 grams	225 grams
16 ounces (1 pound)	455 grams	500 grams (½ kilogram)

Length

Inches	Centimeters
0.5	1.5
1	2.5
2	5.0
3	7.5
4	10.0
5	12.5
6	15.0
7	17.5
8	20.5
9	23.0
10	25.5
11	28.0
12	30.5

Temperature (Degrees)

Fahrenheit	Celsius
32	0
212	100
250	120
275	140
300	150
325	160
350	180
375	190
400	200
425	220
450	230
475	240
500	260

Appendix **B**

Time and Temperature Guide

When cooking barbecue, time and temperature are essential. The following table shows the internal temperature each type of meat needs to reach before it's done and safe to eat.

Internal Meat Temperatures

Meat	Type	Internal Temperature (°F)
Beef, lamb, pork, veal, or a mixture	Ground	160
Fresh beef, lamb, veal	Chops, roasts, steaks	145
Chicken or turkey	Ground	165
Fresh poultry	Whole or any part	165
Fish	Fish with fins	145
Fresh pork	Chops, roasts, and steaks, including ham	145
Precooked ham	To reheat	145

Cook soft-shelled seafood — crab, lobster, scallops, and shrimp — until the flesh is pearly or white and opaque. When the hard shell of clams, mussels, and oysters open, you know they're done cooking.

REMEMBER

In order for brisket, pork shoulder, or pork butt to pull apart for pulled pork, you need an internal temp of 192 degrees. That temperature ensures that the fat renders out and the cartilage breaks down.

Time is also key when it comes to how long it takes meat to reach the necessary internal temperature. The temperature inside your cooker is nearly as important as the internal temperature of your meat. The following table lists my preferred temperature and time ranges.

Time and Temperature Chart

Meat	Temperature	Time
Brisket, pork shoulder, whole hog	200 to 220	12 to 24 hours
Poultry	250 to 275	1½ to 4 hours
Ribs	250	3½ to 5 hours
Beef ribs	250	6 to 8 hours

REMEMBER

The length of time you cook your meat is not as important as the internal temperature. Your meat is done when it's done.

Cooking time is greatly affected by fat content and the shape and size of your cut of meat. Typically, the more fat in a cut, the faster it cooks.

REMEMBER

The internal temperature of the meat stalls at 160 degrees. Don't panic and don't raise the cooking temperature. The stall is the natural process of cooking low and slow. The temperature may stay at 160 degrees for a few hours. Don't worry about it — stay calm and keep smoking.

Index

ham *(continued)*
  overview, 77
  vertical offset smokers, 48
hanger steak (butcher's tenderloin), 228
Hawaiian Marinade, 163
heat
  even distribution of, 60
  indirect, 26–28
    best methods for meats, 27–28
    defined, 13–14
    direct vs., 26–27
  reacting with meat, 22–25, 81
    cooking method, 24–25
    structure and fibers, 25
    what to watch for, 23–24
heat (spicy), 90, 235
Henderson, Tennessee, 11
herbs, 2, 234–236
hickory, 7, 31, 222
high-heat painted steel finish, 41
Honey Lime Watermelon, 209
hoppers, 55
hormones, 66
hot gloves, 36
hot smoking, 21–22
Hungarian paprika, 236
hydrolysis, 25

I

icons
  tomato, 2
  used in this book, 3
Illinois, 239
inches, 245
indirect heat, 26–28
  best methods for meats, 27–28
  defined, 14
  direct vs., 26–27
ingredients, 14–16
  brines, 82–83
    defined, 17, 80
    overview, 30–32
    recipes, 159–161

guidelines for, 2
marinades
  defined, 17, 80
  overview, 83–84
  recipes, 162–164
meat, 15, 16–17, 65–77
  best methods for, 27–28
  butcher shops, 65–66, 227–231
  choosing, 15
  cuts of, 67–77
  heat changing, 22–25
  preparing, 79–86
rubs, 84–86
  basic elements of, 85
  defined, 16–17, 80
  matching to meat, 85–86
  onion powder overpowering, 235
  overview, 30–32
  recipes, 151–157
sauces, 87–92
  adding spices, 91
  balancing, 90–91
  choosing base, 88–90
  experimenting, 91–92
  overview, 87
  recipes, 165–177
  spices, 15–16
injector, brine, 83
insulation, 61
internal meat temperature. *See also* temperature
  chart, 247–248
  general discussion of, 14
  thermometer placement, 224–225
iron wood, 7

J

J&R Manufacturing, 54
jalapeños
  Jalapeño Silver-Dollar Corn Cakes, 182
  Stuffed Jalapeños, 180

Marinade, Steak, 162

Seasoning, Steak, 158

steel

  rods for pits, 57

  walls in grills or smokers, 61

stock pots, 36

stress, 226

strip steak. *See* New York strip

structure of meat, 25

Stuffed Jalapeños, 180

Stuffed Lamb Breast, 128–129

sugar

  burning on meat, 89

  defined, 2

  grilling and, 172

sweet flavor

  allspice, 236

  rub, 85

  sauces, 90

  Sweet Heat BBQ Sauce, 170

  Sweet Tea Brine, 161

T

table salt, 233

tablespoons, 244

tack welding, 61

tacos

  Carnitas Tacos, 144

  Smoked Chicken Tacos, 111

tandoori, 56

Taylor, Texas, 238

T-bone steak, grilling, 71

teaspoons, 244

Tell-Tru, 37

temperature

  with chicken, 105

  consistency with, 14

  conversion guide, 245

  for full combustion, 22

  guidelines for, 247–248

  measurements, 2

  for pulled pork, 131

  stall point, 23, 131, 225

thermometers

  on grills or smokers, 61

  mistakes with, 224–225

  overview, 37–38

temperature control unit, 38

tenderloin steak

  grilling, 71

  hanger steak (butcher's tenderloin), 228

  Smoked Beef Tenderloin, 103

Tennessee

  overview, 11–12

  restaurants, 237, 238, 240

Texas

  overview, 12

  preferred smokers in, 48

  restaurants, 238

texture, fish, 66

thermometers

  on grills or smokers, 61

  mistakes with, 224–225

  overview, 37–38

ThermoWorks, 37

thyme, 236

TIG (tungsten inert gas), 62

timing

  for brining and marinades, 82

  guidelines for, 247–248

  mistakes with, 225–226

tomatoes

  as base, 89

  Grilled Stuffed Tomatoes, 187

  tomato icon, 2

tongs, 23, 38

tools, 33–38

  cooking, 36–38

  for starting fire, 33–36

top feeding smokers, 47

top-cut rib-eye, 71

tough meat, 25, 222

triglycerides, 25

trimming fat, 16

tri-tip

  preferred cooking method for, 27

  Smoked Tri Tip, 100

About the Author

Pitmaster **Carey Bringle** is the owner of the Peg Leg Porker Restaurant and lifestyle brand. As a Nashville native with deep-seated roots in the West Tennessee food and beverage culture, he was born into barbecue. He was raised on iconic West Tennessee barbecue, in which thick smoke, a spicy rub, and a trusty smoker make for a winning combination.

In Carey's family, barbecue is more than eating — barbecue is about bonding and bringing people together. His grandfather, Dr. Carey Bringle, delivered babies for many famous barbecue families in West Tennessee and smoked whole hogs himself. Bruce Bringle, Carey's uncle and mentor, competed in the very first Memphis in May World Championship Barbecue Cooking Contest in 1976, which made quite an impact on Carey. Carey has now competed in that contest for more than 26 years, winning various awards.

At the age of 17, Carey was diagnosed with osteogenic sarcoma, an aggressive bone cancer. After months of intensive chemotherapy, he lost his right leg. Instead of letting this tragedy set him back, he emerged with a new perspective and the realization that every day brings new adventures, new experiences, and another chance to enjoy great food — especially barbecue. It was then that he vowed to place fun, food, friends, and family at the very center of his life.

He opened the Peg Leg Porker Restaurant in 2013 to offer barbecue, sauces, rubs, a new line of professional-grade home smokers, and Peg Leg Porker Tennessee Straight Bourbon Whiskey.

Carey and his restaurant have been featured on television and in magazines since the restaurant doors opened, and Peg Leg Porker has been recognized in prestigious rankings of top barbecue restaurants. Carey has been honored to cook at the prestigious James Beard House in New York City on three separate occasions.

Dedication

I would like to dedicate this book to all of you barbecue enthusiasts out there who will use this book as a tool for your soon-to-be-overwhelming obsession. Barbecue is family, and I'm proud to welcome you all into mine. Barbecue brings us together and should never tear us apart.

Author's Acknowledgments

First, I would like to sincerely thank my family: my wife, Delaniah, and my three children, Carey IV, Connley, and Catherine. You all didn't ask to take this journey with me but have been my inspiration all along. The long hours and time away from you have been hard, but knowing that you all supported my dream unconditionally has made it all worthwhile. I love you all.

My mother, Julia Douglass, has been there for me through good and bad. She has been my rock. When I went through my bout with cancer, she was by my side night and day, even as she worked three jobs as a single mother.

My grandparents on both sides of my family were great stewards of barbecue culture and instilled in me a love for barbecue at a very young age. Gangi and Jack, on my mother's side, and E.G. and Pawpaw, on my father's side, all taught me the importance of barbecue in our culture and community.

My Uncle Bruce and grandfather Jack both allowed me to sit with them at the smoker from a very young age. Their influence is still with me today. They fostered a love for barbecue in me by teaching me all that they knew.

Reed and Kathy and Clay Morgan were next-door neighbors who always went over and above to teach me about work and life. You were always there for me and helped keep me on the path to success. You taught me that I could accomplish anything that I wanted in life.

My first team captains, Ernie Mellor and Tripp Murray, took me in on their team, the Rolling Wonder Pigs, which soon became Hog Wild. They taught me the ropes at Memphis in May and were there for me when I broke off and started my own team.

I thank all of my teammates on the Peg Leg Porkers over the years who I've had the honor of leading. I've learned from every one of you and I've been impressed by how many of you have come into your own in barbecue.

I give thanks for all of my team members at Peg Leg Porker. You've all made great contributions to my success and shown that you're the best in the business. Your dedication to our brand and to me is humbling. It's truly an honor to work with you all.

Last but not least, I'd like to thank my publisher Wiley, specifically Matthew Holt, Tracy Boggier, and Elizabeth Kuball. I'd also like to thank Kathleen Dobie, who took this journey with me and has kept me on track as best she could. You all have been great in your execution of this book.

Publisher's Acknowledgments

Senior Acquisitions Editor: Tracy Boggier
Project Editor: Elizabeth Kuball
Copy Editor: Elizabeth Kuball
Nutrition Analyst: Rachel Nix
Proofreader: Debbye Butler

Production Editor: Mohammed Zafar Ali
Cover Image: © mphillips007 / Getty Images

Leverage the power

Dummies is the global leader in the reference category and one of the most trusted and highly regarded brands in the world. No longer just focused on books, customers now have access to the dummies content they need in the format they want. Together we'll craft a solution that engages your customers, stands out from the competition, and helps you meet your goals.

Advertising & Sponsorships

Connect with an engaged audience on a powerful multimedia site, and position your message alongside expert how-to content. Dummies.com is a one-stop shop for free, online information and know-how curated by a team of experts.

- Targeted ads
- Video
- Email Marketing
- Microsites
- Sweepstakes sponsorship

20 MILLION PAGE VIEWS **EVERY SINGLE MONTH**

15 MILLION UNIQUE **VISITORS PER MONTH**

43% OF ALL VISITORS ACCESS THE SITE **VIA THEIR MOBILE DEVICES**

700,000 NEWSLETTER SUBSCRIPTIONS **TO THE INBOXES OF**
300,000 UNIQUE INDIVIDUALS EVERY WEEK

# of dummies

Custom Publishing

Reach a global audience in any language by creating a solution that will differentiate you from competitors, amplify your message, and encourage customers to make a buying decision.

- Apps
- Books
- eBooks
- Video
- Audio
- Webinars

Brand Licensing & Content

Leverage the strength of the world's most popular reference brand to reach new audiences and channels of distribution.

For more information, visit **dummies.com/biz**

PERSONAL ENRICHMENT

9781119187790	9781119179030	9781119293354	9781119293347	9781119310068	9781119235606
USA $26.00	USA $21.99	USA $24.99	USA $22.99	USA $22.99	USA $24.99
CAN $31.99	CAN $25.99	CAN $29.99	CAN $27.99	CAN $27.99	CAN $29.99
UK £19.99	UK £16.99	UK £17.99	UK £16.99	UK £16.99	UK £17.99

9781119251163	9781119235491	9781119279952	9781119283133	9781119287117	9781119130246
USA $24.99	USA $26.99	USA $24.99	USA $24.99	USA $24.99	USA $22.99
CAN $29.99	CAN $31.99	CAN $29.99	CAN $29.99	CAN $29.99	CAN $27.99
UK £17.99	UK £19.99	UK £17.99	UK £17.99	UK £16.99	UK £16.99

PROFESSIONAL DEVELOPMENT

9781119311041	9781119255796	9781119293439	9781119281467	9781119280651	9781119251132	9781119310563
USA $24.99	USA $39.99	USA $26.99	USA $26.99	USA $29.99	USA $24.99	USA $34.00
CAN $29.99	CAN $47.99	CAN $31.99	CAN $31.99	CAN $35.99	CAN $29.99	CAN $41.99
UK £17.99	UK £27.99	UK £19.99	UK £19.99	UK £21.99	UK £17.99	UK £24.99

9781119181705	9781119263593	9781119257769	9781119293477	9781119265313	9781119239314	9781119293323
USA $29.99	USA $26.99	USA $29.99	USA $26.99	USA $24.99	USA $29.99	USA $29.99
CAN $35.99	CAN $31.99	CAN $35.99	CAN $31.99	CAN $29.99	CAN $35.99	CAN $35.99
UK £21.99	UK £19.99	UK £21.99	UK £19.99	UK £17.99	UK £21.99	UK £21.99

dummies.com

dummies®
A Wiley Brand

Learning Made Easy

ACADEMIC

9781119293576
USA $19.99
CAN $23.99
UK £15.99

9781119293637
USA $19.99
CAN $23.99
UK £15.99

9781119293491
USA $19.99
CAN $23.99
UK £15.99

9781119293460
USA $19.99
CAN $23.99
UK £15.99

9781119293590
USA $19.99
CAN $23.99
UK £15.99

9781119215844
USA $26.99
CAN $31.99
UK £19.99

9781119293378
USA $22.99
CAN $27.99
UK £16.99

9781119293521
USA $19.99
CAN $23.99
UK £15.99

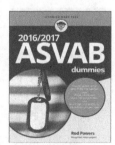

9781119239178
USA $18.99
CAN $22.99
UK £14.99

9781119263883
USA $26.99
CAN $31.99
UK £19.99

Available Everywhere Books Are Sold

dummies.com

dummies®
A Wiley Brand

Small books for big imaginations

9781119177173
USA $9.99
CAN $9.99
UK £8.99

9781119177272
USA $9.99
CAN $9.99
UK £8.99

9781119177241
USA $9.99
CAN $9.99
UK £8.99

9781119177210
USA $9.99
CAN $9.99
UK £8.99

9781119262657
USA $9.99
CAN $9.99
UK £6.99

9781119291336
USA $9.99
CAN $9.99
UK £6.99

9781119233527
USA $9.99
CAN $9.99
UK £6.99

9781119291220
USA $9.99
CAN $9.99
UK £6.99

9781119177302
USA $9.99
CAN $9.99
UK £8.99

Unleash Their Creativity

dummies.com

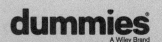